Caribbean East Indian Recipes

About this book

This cookbook represents a comprehensive collection of over 70 "traditional" vegetarian recipes. They have been handed down by our foreparents from India by word of mouth and practical example for over four generations. The food that is now cooked here is distinctly Indo-Caribbean in flavour.

The recipes reveal the secrets of preparing delicious Indian dishes, some of which are unknown to the non-Indian community in the Caribbean.

They cover a wide range of tasty and exciting dishes, from light delightful snacks to dinner - party specials -- from the various types of *rotis, daahls, kuchillas, chutneys, anchars,* sweets and desserts to *chokas* and vegetable *talkaries.*

The recipes have been written in an easy-to-prepare style to be cooked in your own kitchen. The ingredients are readily available at your local grocery store and other food outlets.

Each recipe has been kitchen-tested and, therefore, meets a high standard of accuracy. Some of the dishes are beautifully illustrated in colour to tempt your appetite.

Caribbean East Indian Recipes

Kumar Mahabir

Chakra Publishing House
Tel: (868) 674-6008

Mahabir, Kumar.
Caribbean East Indian Recipes.

First published in 1992 by Chakra Publishing House, Don Miguel
Road, San Juan, Trinidad W.I. Reprinted 2001.

Typesetting and Printing by HEM Enterprises Limited,Trinidad,
West Indies.

ISBN 976-8012-75-7

i. Vegetarian cooking.
ii. Cookery, Caribbean East Indian.
iii. East Indians of the Caribbean.
iv. Title

All photographs (including cover) taken by the author.
E-mail: kumarmahab@hotmail.com
Illustrations by Sundarlal Rampersad.
Illustrations of Edible plants by S.K. Ragbir.

HINDU CREDIT UNION

HCU Group of Companies

FINANCIAL SERVICES

The Flexible FIXED DEPOSIT

BAAL BARAKAT - The Child Starter Plan

The Classic SAVINGS ACCOUNT

Vidya Daan SAVINGS ACCOUNT

INCOME & GROWTH MULTIPLIER FUND

U.S. DOLLARS FLEX ACCOUNT

ATM BANKING

Head Office:
Main Road, Chaguanas.
Tel.:671-3718, 671-5940:
Fax:671-5941

Administrative Center:
151 Edinburgh Village,
Chaguanas.
Tel.:671-4131

Hindu Credit Union Branches

Aranguez Main Road,
San Juan.
Tel./Fax:675-8282

Eastern Main Road,
El Dorado.
Tel./Fax:663-9897

Golden Grove Road,
St. Helena Junction, Piarco.
Tel.:669-4989

Rio Claro Junction, Rio Claro.
Tel.:644-0215

9 Eastern Main Road,
Sangre Grande.
Tel.668-7105

43-45 Frederick St.,
Frederick Court, Port of Spain.
Tel.:627-7752

Tobago, NIB Mall
Tel.: 639-4781

7 Penal Junction, Penal.
Tel.:647-6912, 647-1704/5

Lothians Road, Princes Town.
Tel./Fax:665-8980

St. James Street, San Fernando
Tel.: 653-8098

Southern Main Road, Couva
Tel./Fax:679-7584

15 Guava Road, Point Fortin.
Tel.: 648-3533 / 2513

Other books by Kumar Mahabir

The Still Cry: Personal Accounts of East Indians in Trinidad and Tobago during Indentureship. New York: Calaloux Publications, 1985.

A Dictionary of Common Trinidad Hindi. El Dorado: Chakra Publishing House, 1990.

Medicinal and Edible Plants used by East Indians of Trinidad and Tobago. El Dorado: Chakra Publishing House, 1992.

East Indian Women of Trinidad and Tobago: An Annotated Bibliography with Photographs and Ephemera. San Juan: Chakra Publishing House, 1992.

The Legacy of Indian Indenture: 150 Years of East Indians in Trinidad. New York: Windsor Press, 1995.

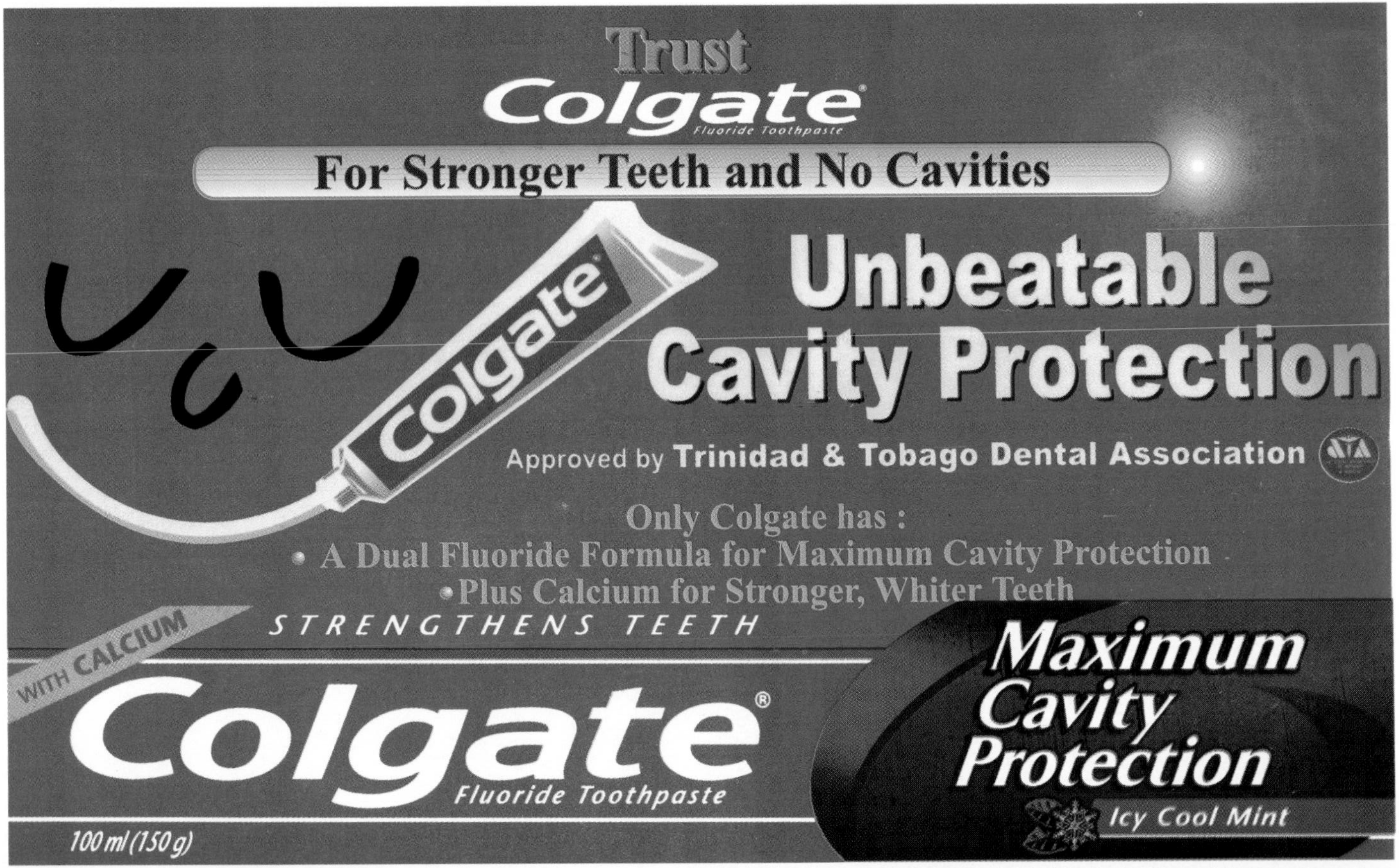
Trust
Colgate
Fluoride Toothpaste
For Stronger Teeth and No Cavities
Colgate
Unbeatable
Cavity Protection
Approved by Trinidad & Tobago Dental Association
Only Colgate has :
• A Dual Fluoride Formula for Maximum Cavity Protection
• Plus Calcium for Stronger, Whiter Teeth
STRENGTHENS TEETH
WITH CALCIUM
Colgate
Fluoride Toothpaste
100 ml (150 g)
Maximum
Cavity
Protection
Icy Cool Mint

For my dear wife, Mera
without whom this book would have been impossible to produce

For all those women (past and present) who passed on to the
younger ones, the art of Indian cooking in the Caribbean

and for Ashraff Ali of Second Hand Book Shoppe who con-
vinced me of the need to write a book like this.

ACKNOWLEDGEMENTS

I would like to thank the members of my "extended" family - Samrajee, Sheila, Kamla, Rajee, Karla, Deomattie, Jaitoon, Krishna, Khemraj, Shanti, Geeta, Tara, Linda, Feroza and Indra - for sharing their knowledge of some dishes with me.

Special appreciation must go to Praimsingh's Pooja Store, "The Indian Connection" for providing me with the brass and silver ornaments used in the photographs, and to Indra Singh for her hand-painted pottery.

My sincere thanks to Kathleen Kassiram for her constructive criticism and her meticulous proofreading at short notice.

Thanks to Gayatri Singh and Rano Toolsiesingh for typing the manuscript.

I am grateful to all those people who gave their comments after tasting all the dishes.

National Pride • Global Standards

QUALITY LUBRICANTS
QUALITY LUBRICANTS
QUALITY LUBRICANTS
QUALITY LUBRICANTS
QUALITY LUBRICANTS
QUALITY LUBRICANTS
QUALITY LUBRICANTS

...the Indians have had a deep effect upon the Caribbean cuisine, primarily through their enthusiasm for curry, which is becoming as much a part of Caribbean as of Indian cooking.

-- Linda Wolfe *et al.* **The Cooking of the Caribbean Islands.** Netherlands: Time-Life International, 1974.

Everything which made the Indian alien in the [Trinidadian] society give him strength. His alienness insulated him from the black-white struggle. He was taboo-ridden as no other person on the island; he had complicated rules about food and about what was unclean.

--V.S. Naipaul. **The Middle Passage.** London: André Deutsch, 1962.

CONTENTS

FOREWORD

Food is very basic. It is necessary for nourishment and human survival. Human beings, like any other living being, get hungry at regular intervals, but in their case its satisfaction is not merely biological. In other words, any food which may provide the necessary nutrition would not do. It has to be a certain food, processed in a particular manner and cooked. Cooking too is not "straight." The food has to be blended with appropriate spices and then boiled or roasted or fried or a combination of them. The final product has to be of a certain shape, texture, colour, flavour and taste and served at the appropriate time of the day. Breakfast food cannot be served as dinner, and dinner cannot be served with afternoon tea. That is, food is associated with the time of the day and it is also usually served in combination with certain food. Style of serving, receptacles in which the food is served, and the implements with which the food is eaten, are also important.

In the process of growing up, one learns what is food and what is non-food; one also learns how the ingredients of food are processed, cut , washed and made ready for normal cooking. Food for ceremonial and ritual occasions could be quite different. Food offered to the dieties may be still different. Food, like many other things in the society, is ranked. High- ranking food is offered to dieties and honoured guests. In most parts of India a son-in-law is considered to be the most honoured guest in a household and, therefore, he is offered the high-ranking food. Food prepared on joyous occasions may be different from that which is prepared on mourning occasions.

In India food prepared during mourning period in a household is bereft of salt, spices, oil and tumeric. Tumeric signifies auspiciousness; its absence indicates inauspiciousness. That is why for all normal and joyous occasions, cooking tumeric is one of the first set of items that is used.

Food is also classified in terms of their attributes; some food are good for health, raise appetite and provide vitality. Some food are supposed to have medicinal properties. Some "cool" the system, while others "heat". All this and much more one learns as a member of a community. Food, thus, is governed by a set of definite norms. These norms evolve over time and we "believe" that these norms are not ad hoc but are integrated with other aspects of society and culture and convey certain meanings to the participants in a culture.

In India, each region has its own food culture. Broadly speaking, northern India is a *roti* region while east and southern regions are rice regions. Within these regions one can identify sub-regions, say on the basis of processing of wheat/rice and cooking them. For instance, in north-western India, the people prefer *tandoori roti* prepared out of wheat dough, rural north-central Indian like to have thick *roti* which is prepared by flattening the dough between the two palms, while the urbanites in the same region like to have thin *roti* called *phulka*. In the eastern region, people like par boiled rice while in other regions people prefer normal white rice. In India food differences are also on caste lines, not only in terms of vegetarianism and non-vegetarianism but also in its processing and cooking. Food prepared in a *kyastha* house is different from the one prepared at the Kshatriya or Brahmin house, not to mention the differences that exist with and between occupational castes. People identify the castes of the household by the aroma emanating from its kitchen. Though the last act in a cycle of cooking a meal in a Hindu house is *chokna* (seasoning), it is highly significant. Of course, it is supposed to enhance the taste of the food, fill the house with a distinct aroma and generate appetite, but it is also meant to announce that the process of cooking is over and the ritual of eating food should begin. *Chokna* is supposed to have a cleansing effect. It is supposed to drive away the evil forces and make room for the *devatas* (dieties) to come and have food. By the time *chokna* is done, the eldest male member of the household should have taken his ritual bath, worn ritually clean clothes, and on hearing the sound of *chokna,* should proceed to the kitchen and offer cooked food to the *devatas* . After this, he and other members of the household are expected to partake the meals. But this too is not simple. There are clear rules as to who can serve what meals and how, both within and outside the house. The concept of ritual purity is an important consideration to determine the status of food and its transactions. Some foods like milk and milk products are pure; their status does not change by cooking and can be transacted across castes and consumed anywhere. Some other foods are not so pure and their status changes by cooking. If such foods are boiled or steamed, their purity becomes extremely vulnerable, and hence can be partaken in the kitchen only when served by the person who is an unequal or of a higher caste and is in a state of ritual purity. If the same items are cooked in oil or *ghee,* they are not so vulnerable and can be consumed outside the kitchen with some restrictions.

Food, thus, merely is not food; it is one of the mediums through which a lot of social, cultural, economic, political and aesthetic messages are communicated. Message communication is an ongoing process; messages are received and decoded for action, and messages are retransmitted. All this takes place in the context of time and space. What happens to the messages and the medium when the context is changed is a matter for serious research. What happened to the Indian food, food-related norms and values in the context of the Indian diaspora? What messages do they convey now? These are relevant questions because the Indians were uprooted from their homeland and brought into a hostile and alien environment. As they were a class of people who were subjected, their traditions were looked down. Except for their labour, they were not supposed to be carrying anything worthwhile. Whatever they had in the name of cultural baggage was to be "reformed". Apart form these external problems, the Indians had their own. They had come form different regions of the country having different traditions. Moreover, all of them had not come at one time; they came in batches and soon after their arrival they were distributed in the different plantations in the country. So first they had to come to terms with the realities of the new life which was imposed on them. How under such conditions the East Indians formed a community and what was the basis of this formation are important sociological questions. In forming a community, they must have searched for those traditions which were unifying and to drop those which were divisive. After all, to form a community and to make the traditions function, an optimum number of people is required. This is particularly relevant when external threat is perceived. Here the external threat was also in terms of conversion to another faith and being continuously looked down by others. Under these circumstances, forgiving alliances across the old identities must have been an urgent issue facing the early immigrants. This led to what can be called a process of churning and inventing traditions on the basis of images of the "home" country to form a homogeneous community. There is plenty of evidence to illustrate that these processes were in operation among the East Indians. However, no process is perfect. In spite of the churning, all the past identities were not dissolved and, in course of time, new identities, new organisations and institutions emerged. Centripetal and centrifugal forces operate simultaneously. In this respect, food is a good and interesting example. It can travel across the groups ignoring their identities and forge unity at another level, but it can become an instrument in itself to mark an identity. Research on food may also indicate what has happened to the society at a much deeper level and to its values.

One may ask as to why such a lengthy introduction to a book on recipes. First, Kumar Mahabir has already established himself as a serious scholar on the Indian diaspora by presenting a number of books on the East Indian in the Caribbean. Second, by this introduction, I wanted to draw the attention of the students of Indian diaspora on the material presented by Kumar Mahabir in this book. It is not only a recipe book, it contains data on Indian food. It gives the information as to what is combined with what and how to produce an item of food. Hitherto, the knowledge of cooking East Indian food has been conveyed through word of mouth. Such oral traditions are of immediate interest to the students of diasporic studies. The book opens up further possibilities of research by asking what is the significance of the combination of various items in preparation of an East Indian food.

Kumar Mahabir's **Caribbean East Indian Recipes** would interest both serious scholars interested in Indian diaspora and also common people. Of course, the serious scholars would like to know how and from where Mahabir collected his information. Mahabir's book gives the impression that there is a great deal of homogeneity in food preparation among the East Indians in the Caribbean. Is it so? This has to be proven by a systematic research rather than assumed.

However, under diasporic conditions, both men and women had to work outside their homes to earn their living. In other words, they had much less time for household chores, particularly cooking. Now both partners working to earn an income has become a norm. It means the role of food to convey the messages has been curtailed to some extent. To that extent, the role of mothers to teach the skills of the culinary must also have been diminished. Thus, the knowledge which was normally transmitted from one generation to another in the process of growing up in a household is not available any longer. Young boys and girls desirous of learning traditional Indian dishes either will have to seek the help of specialist or take the help of the recipe book prepared by Kumar Mahabir. One can see the shift-- what was once within the domestic domain has gone out and has become the domain of a specialist. At the hand of specialist, the folk knowledge of cooking is bound to be more systematised and refined. In the process, the end product will have more wider acceptability, but at the same time its domestic, social and cultural role would have been curtailed. These are speculations which need to be tested by empirical data.

Promode Kumar Misra
Visiting Professor
University of the West Indies
St. Augustine

INTRODUCTION

This is the first book of its kind to be published in the Caribbean. Similar publications attempted by Indian women expatriates, contained largely the styles of cooking that are practised in India rather than the Caribbean. Methods of cooking "traditional" dishes have evolved over four generations since our Indian ancestors first came to these shores as indentured labourers between 1838-1917.

The descendents of these immigrants, who now comprise over one million people in the Caribbean, have found the style of cooking in India to be somewhat different. They observe that those of their ancestral land use clove, *saunf* (aniseed), *hing* (asafoetida), tamarind, bay leaf, *hardi* (tumeric), ginger, *dahee* (yogurt) and chilli powder as part of their daily cooking while, here, they do not. One visiting culinary expert/nutritionist noted that "the islanders do not mix a curry paste for themselves as the Indians do, but always use prepared curry powder" (Wolfe, Linda *et al.* **The Cooking of the Caribbean Islands.** 1979). Tandoori dishes - food cooked on the spit in a clay oven - are foreign to Indo-Caribbean kitchens, but a fair imitation is the now popular barbecue. The influence of Amerindian, Spanish, English, African, French and Chinese cuisine on some of our dishes, and the substitution of locally available items for authentic Indian ingredients, have made the Indian style of cooking unique in the Caribbean.

The social and cultural context in which food was/is prepared and served in the Caribbean provides a fascinating study of cultural persistence and change over space and time. Traditionally, women cooked and served the diners who would sit cross-legged on the floor on a *paal* (length of jute) and eat with their fingers. Women, particularly the daughters-in-law, were supposed to eat only after the men and the children were fed. Women were not expected to eat with their male relatives and even with their husbands. This would be considered disrespectful.

Today the table has turned to a large extent. The ability to cook is not considered a major criterion for marriage and mothers-in-law do not only prepare the meal, but also serve the daughter-in-law if she is a working wife. Some Indian men of the middle and upper class, now assist their wives in cooking without inviting rebuke from elders. But Indian men of all classes would at least help in shredding the chataigne, cutting the mango or chopping the meat. They take full control of the kitchen for grand occasions when plenty of food has to be prepared. Men and women now sit together to dine in their homes and in public places. Indo-Caribbean people have retained the custom of eating with their fingers on sohari leaves - used as disposable plates - for grand dinners, but sitting at the table with china and silverware is now the general practice. The practice of eating *daahl pithee* with a cokeeyeá/coconut leaf-spine, used in as much the same way as the Chinese chop-stick, has disappeared completely as well as the use of enamel tableware.

Nearly all of the taboos relating to caste, religion and ethnicity have been broken down in the Caribbean. The belief persists that food should not be thrown on the ground or swept; leftovers should be given to birds and animals instead of dumping it as garbage. Women who have not yet given birth to children are not allowed to chop pumpkins. Before the 1960s in Trinidad, *dosti roti* ("two-in-one *roti*") was cooked at large Hindu dinners because Hindus associated the now-popular *paratha roti* ("buss-up-shut") with Muslim cuisine. And vegetables which grew on vines were not served at many Hindu weddings. Even up to this day, Muslims cook *daahl* instead of *curhee* (gravy), *mango kuchilla* instead of mango *anchar,* and *aloo* (potato) separately instead of the traditional *channa* (chick pea) and *aloo.*

Hindus still do not eat beef and pork, though it is said that pork is relished by those originally of the lower caste. Muslims do not eat meats if they are not *halaled* (sanctified) and pork not at all. Traditionally, Indians of the Caribbean ate poultry, particularly home-reared chickens - only on Sundays and special occasions. Now meat, fish and poultry are eaten almost every day except by Hindus for the period of 7 to 21 days preceding a religious event. The few Hindus who perform *Dih puja* , in reverence to the land, sacrifice and eat a rooster or hog on the day of the ceremony, and those of the *Kali Mai* (goddess of death and destruction) sect do likewise in their propitiation of her. The meat eaten as a daily meal is often stewed or curried with some kind of vegetable. The Indians who maintain a vegetarian style of eating are few in number, and do so for religious rather than health reasons. With increasing scientific evidence of vegetarian diet on good health and longevity, Indians and non-Indians alike are turning in large numbers to non-meat epicurism. One indication of this is the frequency of Indian food items appearing in Indian folk songs and in the calypsoes sung by Afro-Trinidadian bards. Indeed, some culinary experts claim that the Trinidadian *péleau* has its origin in the Indian *kitchree,* just as yogurt was derived from *dahee.* Commercial home-delivered bread is now also eaten by Indians every day in Trinidad. Indeed, the bakery trade, once dominated by the Chinese and Africans, seems to have been taken over by the Indians.

Indo-Caribbean people have always aspired towards a high degree of cleanliness, particularly in the kitchen. It was not customary to taste (*juta)* food while it was still being cooked, perhaps because it had to be offered to *Agni devata* (the deity of the fire) first. It was even worse to taste food from a spoon which had to be returned to the pot for stirring. Food was not even to be eaten in the kitchen. And women were expected to bathe and tie their hair in an *ohrini* (veil) before preparing any dish. There were special utensils to serve beggars and animals, and even today in most Hindu homes, special utensils are reserved for cooking vegetarian dishes. *Methai* (sweet- meats) were made in the night to avoid the attraction of flies. Traditional Indian families would be hesitant to purchase food for fear of the cook/vendor violating the basic rules of hygiene.

Almost all the tools and implements found in the Western kitchen can be used to prepare Indian food. It is quite remarkable, though, that nearly all the cooking utensils brought by our Indian ancestors one hundred and fifty-four years ago, are still being used today in the Caribbean. The *sil* and *lorha* (grinding stones) are used mainly to grind whole grain *massala* which is used by some cooks in preference for the commercial ground *massala*. The *okhree* and *musar* (mortar and pestle) are also still used today to pound herbs and seasonings. The *puchara* (strips of cloth tied to the end of a stick), used for the basting of *dosti* and *paratha roti,* has no substitute. The *puchara* has become even more popular after one business company in Trinidad used it to promote its brand of baking powder. It is now available at supermarkets and grocery stores. The *chulha* (earthen fireside) is not only used to parch *lawa* (paddy) as one of the rites during the Hindu marriage ceremony, but also to cook food which requires a long cooking time. The *chulha* is in daily use in poverty-stricken Guyana, and in other Caribbean countries it is used as an economical substitute for the gas cooker to boil cow's milk and mature chataigne seeds. The *taria* and *lota* (brass plate and cup) have been retained for use during Hindu ceremonies and to serve those of the Hindu priestly caste in the Caribbean.

The *saphee* (pot-holder made of a pad of jute) is one of the few Indian items that have disappeared in the Caribbean. So too is the soop, made with "tireet" or coconut-branch spines, which has become redundant since there is no reason to *pachuré/ousaawé/patké* (fan) or *beené* (pick) rice anymore on a daily basis. The *simthaa* has decreased in popularity with the *chulah* and its function is accomplished by using the handle of a pot spoon or a spatula to turn the side of the *roti*

Since all of the recipes in this book were handed down by word of mouth and practical example for over four generations in the Caribbean, some of the dishes face the danger of disappearance. For example, *satwa* was made by parching a variety of peas and grains separately and then grinding them together (similar to *chilli bibi*). This flour was placed in a sealed contain-er and carried by those who had to travel long distances. It was eaten a portion at a time by adding sugar and water. *Adowri* is another dish - also used as an ingredient for making *daahl* (gravy) and *talkaris* (any food curried) - that has almost disappeared. It was made from *urdi* (black gram/mung bean) which was soaked, ground with spices and made into balls. *Lai* and *bhélee* were made during sugar cane "crop-time" and sold by vendors. *Lai* was a kind of pop corn made with parched rice and *bhélee* was a round type of sugar-cake. Other dishes which have disappeared altogether are *sara bara* (made with *urdi*, yogurt, cumin, pepper and garlic), *daahl pithee* (a kind of soup made with dumplings), *kuloo* (corn porridge), *goja* (a pie made with grated coconut filling), *choitaa* (a type of quick bread made with flour, baking powder and sugar on a greased baking stone), *san kuchi* (rice boiled with ground provisions) and *dosa roti* (made with rice) which was eaten with coconut *chutney*. *Rasaw*, a kind of soup said to be of south-Indian origin, was drunk principally as a medicine for fevers. It was made from fish, tamarind, *massala*, garlic, black pepper, onion, cumin, mustard seeds and karapulé leaves. This was a unique dish because it contained fish and because it was the only kind of soup to be found in the Indian menu.

Some of the 2,955 (2.6 %) Indians of St. Lucia retain the ritual practice of propitiating the spirits of their ancestors by offering unsalted portions of Indian dishes on a specified day in a *cabé* (hut). The ceremony is referred to as *dinner coolie/ dona coolie/ dine coolie* and the oblations consist of *sohari, daahl puri roti, goolgula, kheer, channa* and *aloo,* mango *anchar* and varieties of *talkari.* The Indians of St. Vincent (5,000 or 5% of the population) have retained much of their traditional dishes (Stone, Linda. "East Indian Adaptations in St. Vincent: Richland Park." 1978). In time, when the Indians of Grenada (10,000 or 11%) have become absorbed by the African population, the only symbol of their presence that would remain is their food. *Roti* has spread itself on the national table and, as in Jamaica, curried goat is relished by non-Indians and is believed to be tastier when prepared by an Indian. A noted nutritionist observed that the Indians and Chinese added a taste for leafy and green vegetables to the Caribbean cuisine. "The Orientals have long been recognised as the finest gardeners in the islands, and in many places, they supply the demand they created for lettuce, cabbage, cucumber and green beans by cultivating and selling them" (Wolfe, Linda. 1979). Even in the smaller islands of Grenada, St. Vincent and St. Lucia, Indians cultivate plots of land - on which cows are reared - to ensure sustenance of their traditional dietary habits.

Of all the Caribbean countries populated by people of East Indian origin, Guyana has maintained most of the cultural traditions. Even today many women do not eat at the homes of their daughters/sons-in-law. *Parsad/prasad/mohan bhog* is not served with all its decorations in a packet as in other countries, but is distributed by handfulls from a wooden tray onto a brown-paper napkin. *Roti* (bread), filled with any kind of *choka* (roasted and pounded vegetable) or *talkari* and tied neatly in a cotton teacloth (made from processed flour bag), is still the preferred sandwich taken for lunch away from home.

Much of the Indian cultural tradition has remained in the other Caribbean islands. Food is still classified as being *satwic* (vegetarian, prepared without spices and pepper), *rajasic* (vegetarian, prepared with spices and pepper) and *thamasic* (non-vegetarian). The first type is used by those of the Hindu priestly caste, while the second and third types --which are often mixed-- are consumed by the majority of Hindus/Indians. Three meals are prepared every day - *roti* for breakfast and dinner, and rice for lunch. Breakfast and dinner are prepared together in the morning if the woman works outside the home. Most Indians take their own lunch to work rather than buy. (At one time, to be seen eating *roti* in a public place was a cause for embarrassment to Indians). A fair number of Indians eat more than one *talkari* or *choka* for a meal with pepper or any kind of *chutney* or *kuchilla* (shredded pickle). All the dishes for a meal including fruit, *methai* and dessert, are served all at once.

The extra food that is cooked every day enhances the Indian's legendary hospitality. Traditionally in the Caribbean, guests were served with *sarbat* (sweetened water) before the meal . Every visitor - even an unexpected one or a beggar - was served before he/she left an Indian home. Today , in Trinidad, announcements are made in the mass media inviting the public to discourses on the *Ramayan* and *Shrimad Bhagawat* where hundreds of guests are served sumptuous meals every night for a week. Friends, relatives and neighbours still contribute in some way to an Indian event held at an individual's home. Before the 1960s in Trinidad when *dosti roti* was popular at Indian dinners, every woman guest carried her *belna* and *chowkee* (rolling pin and bread board) to assist.

Some of the dishes in this book are prepared for special occasions, particularly Hindu weddings, festivals and ceremonies. There is still no school to teach Indian cooking in the Caribbean though community groups and experienced individuals organise classes from time to time. Indian epicurean delight - treated in the same way as Indian music - is still not integrated into the Food and Nutrition course of the Secondary School curriculum in the Caribbean. Cooking techniques, in the main, are passed from mother to daughter and from friend to friend during visits to each other's homes. With the dramatic increase of Indian women's participation in the educational system and in the work place over the decades, generations of women are growing up with little knowledge of preparing the wide range of "traditional" Indian dishes. It is hoped that this book, compiled between 1987 and 1992, will not only fill that gap, but will be used by non-Indians as the point of reference for Indo-Caribbean cuisine.

Every single dish has been kitchen-tested, working with men and women of the Caribbean. Though most of the research was done in Trinidad, the result shows little difference between the food prepared here and that in the other islands. The recipes in this book reflect a basic style of cooking, but they offer considerable scope for experimenting within a given framework. The recipes cover a wide range, from everyday meals to special dishes. The herbs and spices are now widely available at (West) Indian grocery stores and supermarkets even in North America and the United Kingdom. This practical cookbook would no doubt appeal to the novice as well as the experienced cook.

Kumar Mahabir
San Juan, Trinidad
Divali, 1992

WEIGHTS AND MEASURES

It is extremely difficult to give exact working quantities when converting from metric to imperial and vice versa. The metric measurements have been rounded off to the nearest unit of 25 grams. It is important to remember to use either metric or imperial and never try to combine the two as they are not exactly equivalent and, therefore, not interchangeable. Spoon measures can be bought in both imperial and metric sizes to give accurate measurements of small quantities.

When converting quantities over 20 ounces, first add the approximate figures in the centre column, then adjust to the nearest unit of 25. As a general guide, 1 kilogram (1000 grms) equals 2.2 lbs or about 2 lbs 3 ozs.

SOLD MEASURES

OUNCE	APPROX. GRAMS TO NEAREST WHOLE	RECOMMENDED CONVERSION TO
1	28	25
2	57	50
3	85	75
4	113	100
5	142	150
6	170	175
7	198	200
8	227	225
9	255	250
10	283	275
11	312	300
12	340	350
13	368	375
14	396	400
15	425	425
16	454	450

LIQUID MEASUREMENTS

IMPERIAL	AMERICAN	APPROX MLS TO NEAREST WHOLE FIGURE	RECOMMENDED MLS
¼ pt	2 /3 cups	142	150
½ pt	1¼ cups	283	300
¾ pt	2 cups	425	450
1 pt	2½ cups	567	600
1½ pts	3¾ cups	851	900
1¾ pts	3½ cups	992	1,000

ABBREVIATIONS

lb / lbs   pound/s
oz / ozs   ounce/s
ml / mls   millilitre/s
tsp / tsps   teaspoon/s
pt / pts   pint/s
grm / grms   gram/s
min / mins   minute/s

PRAYER BEFORE MEALS

Om Brahma pranam Brahma havih Brahma agnau	The offering is to God. God is the offering. The offering is made into the fire which is God.
Brahma hutam Brahmaivatena gantavyam	The offering is made by God. God alone is the One to whom the offering is made.
Brahma karma samadhina Om visvatma priyatam	When seen through samadhi, all this action is of God. May the Universal Self be satisfied.
Om tat sat	That alone is true and real.
Brahma pranam astu	The offering is to God.
Om shanti shanti shanti	May there be peace, peace peace.

O God, bless this food so that it brings vitality and energy
to fulfill Thy mission and serve humanity.
O God, bless this food so that we remain aware of Thee
within and without.
O God, bless this food so that we love all and exclude none.
Bless those who have provided this food, who have
prepared this food, and who will eat this food.
Bless all, my Lord. Amen.

HERBS, SPICES AND SEASONINGS USED IN CARIBBEAN EAST INDIAN COOKING

Aromatics - spices, herbs and seasonings - are at the very heart of Indian cooking. The use of aromatics, combined with the techniques and styles of cooking, gives Indian cuisine its unique character. Flowers, leaves, roots, bark, seeds and bulbs are used in various combinations to produce a variety of flavours: sweet, sharp, hot, sour, spicy, tart, mild, fragrant or pungent.

The aromatics are used to enhance the flavour of the food without masking the taste of the basic ingredients or minimising their nutritive value. If used in moderation, they stimulate appetite and promote good health; but the secret of their successful use is knowing their right combinations and proportions.

All spices must be stored in airtight containers in a cool, dry place as they tend to loose their freshness if exposed too long to air, heat or moisture. Wherever possible, spices should be bought "whole" and ground at home for immediate use. It is advisable to use fresh herbs to give a more concentrated and stronger flavour.

All the ingredients in the recipes are available in (West) Indian specialty food stores and supermarkets.

cardamom (*Elychee/illaichi/elaichi*) Cardamom is a fragrant and disgestive spice used extensively in Indian cookery. A family to the ginger, cardamom is the world's most expensive spice after saffron. The dried fruit consists of 3 capsules containing tiny seeds. The pod is about the size of a large pea and may be buff-coloured if it is bleached, green if dried in an oven; or brown if dried in the sun. The pod itself is not used in cooking but is broken to get the seeds inside. The pungent somewhat lemon-like flavour is most pronounced in the seed of the green cardamom. The seeds of 4 whole pods measure approximately ¼ teaspoon. In Trinidad, the powdered form of cardamom is available at most *puja* stores.

cinnamon (*Dal chini*) It is made from a brown bark peeled from a tree of the evergreen family. Cinnamon adds an aromatic and warm flavour to food. It is available as a powder and in stick rolls.

chive Chive is a hardy perennial herb resembling a fine-leaved onion. Unlike the onion, to which it is related, its stalks and leaves are edible and used as seasoning and garnish in cooking.

clove (*Laung/luong*) Cloves are the dried flower buds of an evergreen of the myrtle family. It is used not only in cookery but also to sweeten the breath and relieve the pain of toothache. They contain a mild anaesthetic and are better when bought whole and not in powdered form.

cumin (*Geera/zeera*) The seeds are long and slim and resemble caraway, but are slightly bitter in taste. They have a distinct warm aroma. Cumin is added to curried dishes and *garam massala* for flavouring and preserving. Whole seeds are used in *daahl* (yellow lentil)

curry Curry powder is a mixture of different spices, the flavour being achieved through the combination of the aromatic oils that the individual spices possess. Curry powder usually includes a combination of ground cumin, chilli powder, coriander, tumeric, ginger, cardamom and *garam massala*. It is easily available at Indian specialty shops, super-markets and in the market place.

fenugreek   (*Methi*) It belongs to the spinach family. The seeds are hard and chunky. The taste and aroma are released only by cooking. Rich in Vitamin C and iron, it is small and rectangular in shape and dark yellow in colour. It is rather bitter in taste and should, therefore, be used sparingly.

garlic   (*Lahsun*) Garlic is a natural antibiotic cleanser rich in iron . This precious bulb adds flavour to some foods. The size of the bulbs varies consid-erably as does the number of cloves to the bulb. It is considered a cure for many diseases.

ginger   (*Adrak*) Ginger is an underground stem or rhi-zome, native to tropical Asia. It is available fresh or dried. The light-brown gnarled root of the fresh ginger is used in Indian and Oriental cooking and has to be peeled, chopped or grated before use. It has quite a hot pungent flavour and should be used sparingly. Ginger has medicinal properties.

karapulé   (*Karapeelé/metha-neem/curry-leaf tree*) These are small grey-greenish leaves with a strong smell. They can be used fresh or dried as seasoning, but are a standard ingredient to *talkari*. The leaves are used to make *chutney*.

lovage   (*Ajwain/jawine*) A member of the liquorice fami-ly, *ajawin* is a powerful, hot spice to be used in moderation. It has medicinal properties and is of-ten used for stomach cramps.

massala	A mixture of spices and other seasonings ground together. The people of the Caribbean feel that *massala* has a richer flavour when the whole grains are ground at home. It is usually sautéd before the main ingredients of a dish are added to the pot.
mint	*(Podina/pudeena)* An aromatic herb used in *talkaris* and for garnishing.
mung bean	Black gram *(urdi)* is an erect or sub-erect, diffusely branched annual herb occasionally trailing with reddish-brown hairs. The seeds are ground and used in the making of *bara* and *saheena.*
mustard oil	A yellow oil derived form the seeds of the mustard plant, used especially for pickling (for *anchar, kuchilla,* etc.). It contains manganese and vitamin D and is pungent in flavour.
nutmeg	*(Jaiphal)* It is preferred that these are bought whole and grated fresh at home. This pungent spice is used to flavour milk dishes, pickles and sweetmeats and is also used as a seasoning.
onion	*(Pyaaz)* A flavouring used in *talkaris* and side dishes. It contains vitamin D and sulpur.
rose water	This is a liquid flavouring distilled from fresh rose petals. It is available in pharmacies as well as Oriental specialty stores.
saffron	*(Zafran/kesar)* One of the most expensive of flavourings, and often what is sold as saffron is not saffron. Seventy-five thousand crocus flowers are needed to make one ounce of pure saffron. It

gives an exquiste flavour and a matchless aroma, and is used as a colouring agent. Only a pinch is required. In the Caribbean, it is substituted with tumeric *(hardi)* which is cheaper.

shado beni   *(Bandhaniya/*fit weed)   A much-branched, prostrate, biennial pungently scented herb which has become the standard ingredient in all *talkaris* and *chutneys* prepared by Indians of the Caribbean.

split peas   Yellow type *(Daahl)* This is the Hindi name given to all members of the legume or pulse family. They are available in cans and as dried beans, peas or lentils. These include chick peas *(channa)* and yellow lentils *(moong)*. Pre-soaking usually cut their cooking time by half and, as salt tends to harden pulses, it should not be added until the end of the cooking.

tamarind   *(Imli)* These are the ripe pods of a large tropical tree which are filled with a dark red juicy pulp that has a souring effect. The seeds and pods are discarded after the pulp has been extracted. It has a very tart citric flavour.

tumeric   *(Hardi/haldi)* This is a tropical Asian plant belonging to the ginger family. The saffron-yellow ground form is commonly used. It is sometimes used to colour food and has a distinctive flavour. It is advisable to buy the root which can be pounded finely before immediate use. The boiled, grounded stems are used to purify, cleanse and lighten the skin.

See key on next page.

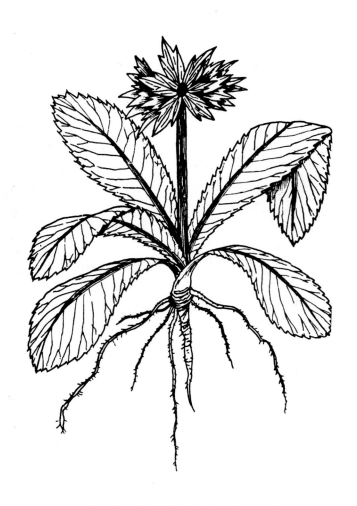

Bandhaniya / shado beni / fit weed

Key to last page
1.Karapulé 2.Clove 3.Tille 4.Curry powder 5.Chive 6.Cinnamon sticks 7.Nutmeg 8.Ginger 9.Methi 10.Elychee 11.Onion 12.Garlic 13.Hot pepper 14.Podina 15.Whole grain massala 16.Tumeric powder 17.Cumin seeds

Rotis
(Breads)

Aloo Roti

This type of roti, *also referred to as* "aloo puri", *is not popular in India. In the Caribbean, it is prepared and eaten at home as a meal in itself with any kind of* chutney.

Ingredients
1½ lbs / 675 grms sifted white flour
½ lb / 225 grms white flour (for *partan*)
4 tsp / 4 x 5 ml spoon baking powder
2 tsp / 2 x 5 ml spoon vegetable oil
3/4 pt / 450 mls water (to knead flour)
½ pt / 300 mls vegetable oil
Pinch of salt

Filling
2 lbs / 900 grms *aloo* (potatoes)
2 tsp / 2 x 5 ml spoon ground *geera* (cumin)
2 large cloves garlic (minced)
1 hot pepper (optional)
¾ pt / 450 mls water
Salt to taste

Method
- Combine 1½ pounds flour, baking powder and salt in a large mixing bowl.
- Knead flour with water to make a soft dough.
- Work in 2 teaspoons vegetable oil into the dough, cover and leave to rest for 30-35 minutes.
- Meanwhile, peel, wash and cut potato into small cubes.
- Boil potato in ¾ pint water until tender and drain.
- Mash potato, add salt, pepper, garlic and ground *geera*.
- Mix thoroughly and set aside.
- Make 10 *loyahs* with dough and leave to rest for 10 minutes.
- Roll out *loyahs* about 3" in diameter with *belna*.

2

- Fill each *loyah* with 2 - 3 tablespoons potato filling.
- Bring over edges to cover potato filling, keeping ball shape
- Leave to rest for 5 - 10 minutes.
- Heat *tawa* and spread a little oil with a *puchara*.
- Roll out *loyahs* about 6 " in diameter on a floured flat surface.
- Cook on *tawa,* basting *roti* on both sides with oil.
- When it "balloons"out and is slightly brown, remove from *tawa.*

Variations

A similar dish is made in India and is called *"alu paratha."* It is served warm and is traditionally accompanied by plain *dahi* (yogurt).

kalchul

3

Cassava Roti

Two generations ago, this type of roti *was commonly eaten by Indo-Caribbean peoples.*

Ingredients
1 lb / 450 grms fresh cassava
4 tsp / 4 x 5 ml spoon brown sugar
8 ozs / 225 grms sifted white flour
2 tsp / 2 x 5 ml spoon baking powder

Method
•Peel, wash and grate cassava.
•Add flour and mix thoroughly in a bowl.
•Mix in brown sugar and baking powder.
•Divide mixture into 8 equal portions to make 8 *loyahs* (balls).
•Heat *tawa.*
•Flatten each *loyah* with palm of hands (about 4-6" in diameter) and cook on both sides on *tawa* on medium heat until it turns light brown. (Use a knife to lift and turn roti).

Serve hot.

Variations
If commercial cassava flour is being used, add water to make dough.

Daahl Puri Roti

This is the tastiest of all the varieties of roti, *though it takes a longer time to prepare. It is served on special Indian occasions with* talkari *cooked with plenty of sauce /gravy.*

Ingredients

For filling
1 lb /450 grms yellow *daahl* (split peas)
1 head garlic (minced)
1 tsp / 1 x 5 ml spoon *hardi* (tumeric)
2 tsp / 2 x 5 ml spoon ground *geera* (cumin)
2 pts / 1200 mls water
Salt to taste

For roti mixture
2 lbs / 900 grms sifted white flour
4 tsp / 4 x 5 ml spoon baking powder
½ tsp / ½ of 5 ml spoon salt
2 tsp /2 x 5 ml spoon vegetable oil
¼ litre / 250 mls vegetable oil
1 pt / 600 mls water (to knead flour)

Method
●Wash *daahl* and drain.
●Cook *daahl* with *hardi* for about 15-20 minutes until *daahl* grain crushes easily between thumb and forefinger. (*Daahl* should not melt.)
●Grind *daahl* on a *sil* (flat stone) or in a hand mill.
●Combine the garlic, *geera,* salt and *daahl* in a large bowl and set aside.
●Mix flour with baking powder and salt.
●Knead with water to make a soft dough.

- Leave dough to rest for 30-45 minutes.
- Cut dough into 15 equal pieces.
- Make 15 small *loyahs* (balls) and leave to rest for 15 minutes.
- Flatten each *loyah* a little and put 2-3 heaped tablespoons *daahl* mixture in the centre of each circle.
- Fold over edges to cover *daahl,* keeping ball shape.
- Roll out dough to about 8" in diameter and place on a hot *tawa* (baking stone), cooking each side in turn.
- Paste a little vegetable oil (about ¾ tablespoon) on both sides of the *roti* using a *puchara*
- *Roti* is cooked when it rises (like a balloon) and is light brown in colour.

Variations

In Guyana, lard is mixed into the dough and less cooking oil is used. Whole wheat flour is sometimes substituted for the white flour.

Dosti Roti

This type of roti *is cooked and eaten hot at home by Indians for breakfast or dinner. It is sometimes referred to as"two-leaf* roti*."*

Ingredients
1¾ lbs /800 grms white flour
4 ozs /100 grms white flour (for *partan*)
4 tsp / 4 x 5 ml spoon baking powder
2 tsp / 2 x 5 ml spoon vegetable oil
Approx. 5/8 pt /375 mls water
Vegetable oil for basting *roti*
Pinch of salt

Method
•Sift flour and baking powder.
•Add salt and mix in thoroughly.
•Make a soft dough using the water.
•Work in 2 teaspoons vegetable oil into the dough.
•Leave to rest for 30-45 minutes.
•Cut dough into 8 - 10 equal pieces.
•Shape into *loyahs* (balls) and leave to rest for another 15 minutes.
•Flatten two *loyahs,* each about 3 " in diameter.
•Sprinkle flour on one side of one *loyah* and paste oil on the other.
•Join the two (like two slices of bread when making a sandwich), placing the side with the flour against the side with the oil.
•Heat *tawa* (baking stone) and roll out *loyahs* to about 7 " in diameter.
•Place on *tawa* and cook on both sides basting a little vegetable oil (on both sides) using a *puchara.*
•Cook until light brown.
•Remove from *tawa* and split open.

Variations

Some cooks add *ghee* (clarified butter) or margarine to make a tastier *roti*.

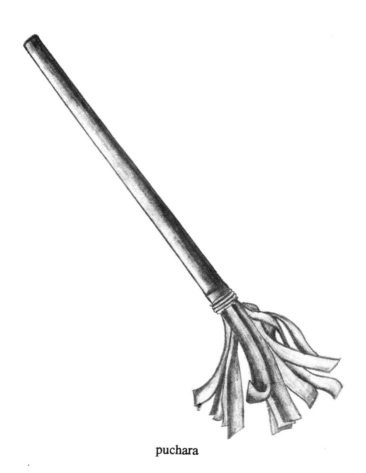

puchara

Paratha Roti

This type of roti *is known as "buss-up-shut" in Trinidad because of its resemblance to a bursted-up shirt. It is available at many Indian food outlets, some of which offer a catering service for weddings and other occasions.* Paratha roti *is enjoyed by Indians and non-Indians alike.*

Ingredients

8 cups 2 lbs /900 grms white flour   4 cups
6 tsp /6 x 5 ml spoon baking powder   3 tsp / 1 tbls
1 cup 4 pot spoons / 200 mls vegetable oil or *ghee* (clarified butter) ½ cup
2 tsp / 2 x 5 ml spoon vegetable oil   1 tsp
3 ozs /75 grms margarine   ⅛ pot Earth Balance
1½ pts / 900 mls water (to knead flour)   2½ cups
Pinch of salt

Method

- Sift flour in a large mixing bowl.
- Take out 4 ounces flour and set aside for *parthan* (dry flour to sprinkle).
- Combine flour, baking powder and salt.
- Knead with water to make a soft dough.
- Smear dough lightly all over with 2 teaspoons oil.
- Leave to rest for about 2 hours.
- Divide dough into 6 equal parts and make into *loyahs* (balls).
- Roll out *loyah* with a *belnaa* on lightly floured board into a circle 5" in diameter and ¼" thick.
- Paste a little margarine to cover surface completely.
- Sprinkle a little flour.
- Cut a straight line from the centre to one end.
- Roll the end with hand in clockwise direction making a cone shape. (Same method when making a croissant).
- Tuck in both ends and press flat.
- Leave to rest for 30 minutes.

9

- Put *tawa* (baking stone) to heat.
- Mix *ghee* and oil in a bowl.
- Roll out *loyahs* on floured board, to about 1/8 " thick, and cook on *tawa*, turning both sides and basting with oil and *ghee* mixture with a *puchara*.
- Place on a clean kitchen cloth and "pound up" with hands or end of *belnaa* until partially broken up into strips.

Serves 6-8 persons.

Variations
Some cooks who prefer a richer *paratha roti*, use only the ghee and butter (and exclude the oil). Evaporated milk can be substituted for, or combined with, the water to knead the flour.

1.Curried aloo 2.Daahl puri roti 3.Baigan Choka 4.Mango Kuchilla 5.Sada roti 6.Tomato choka
7.Barfee

A man cooks *paratha roti* ("buss-up-shut") on a large *tawa* (platen)
over an open fire.

Roat

This unique type of Indian pancake is prepared only for Hanuman puja *(Hindu ceremonial worship in praise of god of the wind). It is broken up into pieces and offered as an oblation and then to the guests.*

Ingredients
8 ozs / 225 grms sifted white flour
6-8 ozs / 175-225 grms brown sugar
1/3 pt / 200 mls chilled evaporated milk
4 tsp / 4 x 5 ml spoon *ghee* (clarified butter)
4 ozs / 100 grms *ghee* (to fry *roat*)

Method
• Dissolve sugar in milk and set aside.
• Sift flour in mixing bowl.
• Rub in 4 teaspoons *ghee* with flour.
• Knead flour with milk mixture to make fairly stiff dough.
• Leave to rest for 5-10 minutes.
• Divide dough into 10 small balls.
• Heat 4 ounces *ghee* in an iron pot.
• Flatten balls with hands (to resemble a pattie) and fry on low heat until golden brown.

Makes 10 roat.

Sada roti

This type of roti is eaten by Indians at home almost everyday at breakfast. It is, however, hardly known and/or eaten by non-Indians as it is only now being made available at fast food outlets. It is eaten with choka *(roasted or pounded vegetable) and/or any kind of* talkari *(curried dish).*

Ingredients
1 lb /450 grms white flour
4 tsp / 4 x 5 ml spoon baking powder
½ pt /300 mls water
½ tsp / ½ of 5ml spoon vegetable oil
Pinch of salt

Method
- Sift flour into a fairly large mixing bowl.
- Add baking powder and salt and mix in thoroughly.
- Knead flour with water to make smooth, soft dough.
- Pour oil in the palm of your hands and paste over dough.
- Leave dough to rest for 10-15 minutes.
- Divide dough into four equal parts and shape into *loyahs* (balls).
- Leave to rest for another 10-15 minutes.
- Put *tawa* (baking stone/platen) to heat on a medium fire.
- Using a *belnaa* (rolling pin), roll out dough, about 6 mm / ¼" thick and round, taking care to make the edges thin.
- Lay out on *tawa* to cook.
- Turn with pot holders, preferably the mitten type.
- Toast edges over fire to make sure they are cooked.
- Keep turning on both sides until brown.

Serves 4-6 persons.

14

Variations

Most people claim that when *sada roti* is cooked over a *chulha* (open fire), it is tastier. It is, however, more convenient nowadays to cook it over a gas flame.

tawa

Sohari

Sohari *is prepared especially for* Durga puja *(Hindu ceremonial worship in praise of an aspect of the Divine Mother). In Guyana, this small fried pancake is called "puri" and is made in large quantities and served to guests during grand Indian functions.*

Ingredients
4 ozs / 100 grms white flour
1 tsp / 1 x 5 ml spoon *ghee* (clarified butter)
2-3 ozs / 50-75 grms *ghee* (to fry)
1 pot spoon / 50 mls water

Method
•Sift flour in mixing bowl.
•Rub in *ghee.*
•Knead mixture with water to make soft dough.
•Divide dough into 5 equal parts and make 5 *loyahs* (balls)
•Heat 2 - 3 ounces *ghee* until piping hot
•Roll out *loyahs* thinly (about 4" in diameter) on a flat, floured surface.
•Fry in *ghee* for ½ minute on each side. (Do not allow to get brown).

Makes 5 *sohari.*

Serve with *lupsee* and /or *kheer* (sweet rice / rice pudding).

Daahl
(Pulses and Legumes)

Curried Channa (Chick peas) and Aloo (Potato)

This dish is very popular in the menu at Hindu weddings and pujas. *It is usually eaten with any kind of* roti.

Ingredients.
1 lb /450 grms *channa* (chick peas)
1 lb /450 grms *aloo* (potato)
5 leaves minced *bandhaniya* (shado beni)
2 tsp /2 x 5 ml spoon *anchar massala*
4 tsp /4 x 5 ml spoon curry powder
1 tsp /1 x 5 ml spoon whole grain *geera* (cumin)
1 tsp /1 x 5 ml spoon baking powder
1 tsp /1 x 5 ml spoon vegetable oil
2 pot spoons /100 mls vegetable oil
1 tsp / 1 x 5 spoon *hardi* (tumeric)
1 tsp /1 x 5 ml spoon ground *geera*
4 pts /2400 mls water (for boiling *channa*)
8 tsp /8 x 5 ml spoon water (to mix curry)
2 large blades chives
1 pt / 600 mls water
1 small diced onion (optional)
1 clove garlic (minced)
1 head garlic (minced)
Salt to taste

Method
- Soak *channa* overnight in 1 pint water.
- Wash *channa,* drain and rub in baking powder and 1 teaspoon of oil.
- Put 4 pints water to boil.
- Add *channa.* Skim foam-like substance from the top and discard.
- Allow to cook until tender.
- Peel and wash *aloo.*

- Cut into small cubes 1" thick.
- Wash and chop chive finely and dice onion.
- Heat 2 pot spoons oil in a medium- sized iron pot.
- Add whole grain *geera* and 1 crushed clove of garlic.
- Mix curry powder, chive, *hardi,* onion, *bandhaniya* and rest of garlic with 8 teaspoons of water.
- Add to hot oil.
- Fry for 2 - 3 minutes.
- Add *aloo* and fry for 2 minutes, stirring frequently.
- Add *channa,* water and salt and cook together until *aloo* is soft.
- Mix in ground *geera* and *anchar massala.*

Serves 8-10 persons.

Variations
In India, blanched ripe tomatoes and tamarind are added to the ingredients. The dish is called "aloo chole" or "alu matter."

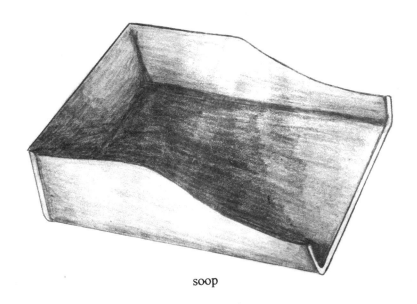

soop

19

Curhee

This dish is served hot during grand Indian occasions and is usually eaten with rice.

Ingredients
½ lb / 225 grms ground *daahl* (split peas)
7/8 pt / 500 mls water
3 ½ pts / 2100 mls hot water
2 pot spoons / 100 mls vegetable oil
10 tsp / 10 x 5 ml spoon water
2 tsp / 2 x5 ml spoon *hardi* (tumeric)
1 large head garlic (minced)
6 large leaves *bandhaniya* (shado beni)
2 tsp / 2 x 5 ml spoon ground *geera*
Salt to taste

For poran
1 bundle chive (washed and finely chopped)
1 tsp / 1 x 5 ml spoon minced garlic
1 tsp / 1 x 5 ml spoon whole grain *geera* (cumin)
1 hot pepper
1 onion finely diced

Method
- Prepare some *phulowrie*. (See recipe for *phulowrie*).
- Combine ground *daahl* and 7/8 pint water.
- Mix well and set aside.
- Heat oil.
- Add 1 teaspoon garlic, chive, *geera* and onion and fry until brown.
- Mix *hardi* with 10 teaspoons water and add to pot.
- Add rest of garlic and *bandhaniya*.
- Fry all the ingredients for 3-5 minutes.
- Stir in *daahl* mixture and whole pepper.
- Add hot water and salt and keep stirring.

•Cook for 45 minutes.
•Mix in the ground *geera* and add *phulowrie.*

Serves 10 - 12 persons.

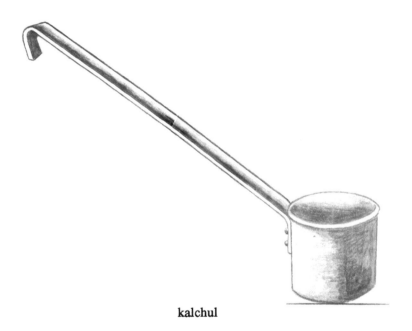

kalchul

Daahl (Yellow split peas)

Daahl *is eaten mainly with boiled rice, but sometimes with* roti
*(flat bread). It was the basic staple diet of Indians until the last
decade.*

Ingredients
1 lb /450 grms yellow split peas
1 tsp / 1 x 5 ml spoon vegetable oil
6 tsp / 6 x 5 ml spoon vegetable oil (to *chownkay*)
1 tsp /1 x 5 ml spoon baking powder
2 tsp /2 x 5 ml spoon *hardi* (tumeric) powder
2 large cloves crushed garlic
1 tsp /1 x 5 ml spoon whole grain *geera* (cumin)
3 pts / 1800 mls water
3 pts / 1800 mls water (to soak *daahl)*
Salt to taste.

Method
• Pick and wash split peas.
• Soak in 3 pints water for about 1 hour before cooking.
• Put 3 pints water to boil.
• Wash split peas again and drain water.
• Add baking powder and 1 teaspoon oil to split peas and rub in
  with hands.
• Add to boiling water.
• Skim froth (until there is none left).
• Add *hardi* and half of the garlic.
• Cook for about 25-35 minutes.
• Swizzle *daahl* with a *daahl ghotnee* (wooden swizzle stick)
  until *daahl* grains have melted.
• Heat 6 teaspoons oil in a *kalchul* (ladle) or in a deep pot spoon.
• Add whole grain *geera* and rest of garlic to hot oil.
• When garlic turns golden brown, remove from fire.
• Add to *daahl,* making sure to keep pot covered.

• Stir well before serving.

Variations

In South India, chopped tomatoes, onions, ginger and *bandhani-ya* (shado beni) are added to the ingredients. *Daahl* made from lentils, is an important part of the basic diet of India.

daahl ghotnee

Googanie

This snack is tastier when eaten with pepper sauce. It is popular at bars in Trinidad where it is sold to the men during their drinking sessions.

Ingredients
1 lb /450 grms black eye peas or fresh pigeon peas
2 tsp /2 x 5 ml spoon minced garlic and *bandhaniya*
1 pot spoon /50 mls vegetable oil
2 pts /1200 mls water (to pre-soak black eye peas)
3 pts /1800 mls water (to boil black eye peas)
1 small onion (diced)
Salt to taste
Hot pepper to taste

Method
•Pick, wash and soak black eye peas in 2 pints water for about 1 hour.
•Put the rest of water to boil.
•Drain black eye peas and add to boiling water.
•Add salt.
•Cook until soft.
•Drain peas in collander/strainer.
•Heat oil in an iron pot.
•Add onion, *bandhaniya,* pepper and garlic and sauté for 1 minute.
•Mix in black eye peas, turning briskly for about 2 minutes.

Serves 6-8 persons.

Kitchree

This is a quick, economical and easy-to-prepare dish that would add colour to your dining table. It is tastier when eaten with grated mango or pomme cythere chutney.

Ingredients
½ lb / 225 grms yellow *daahl* (split peas)
1¾ lbs / 775 grms brown rice
4 pts / 2400 mls water
2 pts / 1200 mls water (to soak *daahl*)
4 tsp / 4 x 5 ml spoon minced garlic
2 tsp / 2 x 5 ml freshly ground *bandhaniya* (shado beni)
1 tsp / 1 x 5 ml *hardi* (tumeric)
1 small onion (diced)
Salt to taste

To chownkay
1 tsp / 1 x 5 ml spoon minced garlic
1 pot spoon / 50 mls vegetable cooking oil

Method
•Pick, wash and soak *daahl* for 30-45 minutes in 2 pints water.
•Put 4 pints to boil in a large iron pot.
•When water is hot, wash *daahl* and add to pot.
•Add *hardi* and turn pot.
•Wash rice and add to *daahl* when it is half-cooked.
•Add garlic, salt, onion and *bandhaniya*.
•Cook until rice is soft and until water is absorbed.
•Heat oil in a *kalchul* and add 1 teaspoon garlic.
•Add to rice and stir in thoroughly.

Serves 6 persons.

Variations
In South India, cloves and diced potatoes are added to the given ingredients The dish is called *"kichadi."* In Guyana, chipped green plantains are added to the two (2) main ingredients of *daahl* and rice.

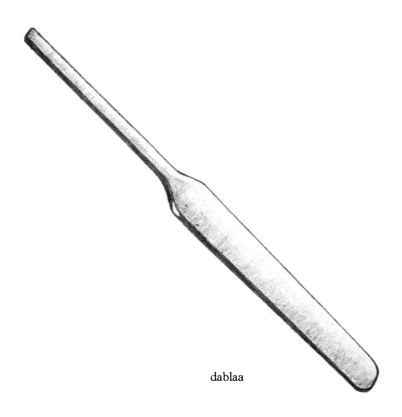

dablaa

Sabji (Vegetables) and Talkari

Aloo Choka

Aloo choka *was the basic dish served with* sada roti *or rice and* daahl *at the homes of poor Indian families.*

Ingredients
1 lb / 450 grms *aloo* (potato)
1 onion (finely diced)
2 cloves garlic (minced)
2 tsp / 2 x 5 ml spoon vegetable oil
2 pts / 1200 mls water
1 hot pepper
Salt to taste

Method
• Peel and wash *aloo*.
• Cook in 2 pints water until tender.
• Drain in collander.
• Mash *aloo* in bowl and add salt.
• Mix in oil, garlic, onion and hot pepper.

Serves 3-4 persons.

Variations
You can *chownkay* the *choka* by heating the oil in a *kalchul* and adding the onion. When the onion is brown, add oil to *choka* and mix in thoroughly Eddoes and "fig" (green banana) *choka* can be made by substituting them for *aloo*.

Baigan and Aloo (Eggplant and Potato)

This is just one of the methods to prepare baigan . *This dish is usually served with hot* sada *or* dosti roti *and mango* anchar *or* kuchilla.

Ingredients
1½ lbs / 675 grms *baigan* (melongene/eggplant)
1½ lbs / 675 *aloo* (potatoes)
2 pot spoons /100 mls vegetable oil
1 tsp /1 x 5 ml spoon whole grain *geera* (cumin)
1 tsp /1 x 5 ml spoon minced garlic
4 tsp /4 x 5 ml spoon minced garlic and *bandhaniya* (shado beni)
4 tsp / 4 x 5 ml spoon curry powder
1 tsp / 1 x 5 ml spoon ground *geera*
8 tsp / 8 x 5 ml spoon water (to mix curry)
2½ pts / 1500 mls hot water
1 hot green pepper
Salt to taste

Method
•Wash, peel and cut up *aloo* in small cubes.
•Wash, peel and cut up *baigan* into small pieces.
•Place in a dish with enough water to cover and soak for a few minutes. (This prevents discolouration of the *baigan* and *aloo*).
•Heat oil in a large iron pot
•Mix curry powder, garlic, and *bandhaniya* with 8 teaspoons water and set aside.
•Add the whole grain *geera* and 1 teaspoon minced garlic to hot oil.
•When garlic is brown, stir in curry mixture and fry well for about 1 minute.
•Drain *baigan* and *aloo* and add to curry mixture.
•Fry for 3 - 4 minutes.

- Add salt, hot pepper and hot water and stir.
- Add ground *geera* when *baigan* and *aloo* are soft and mushy.

Serves 6 -8 persons.

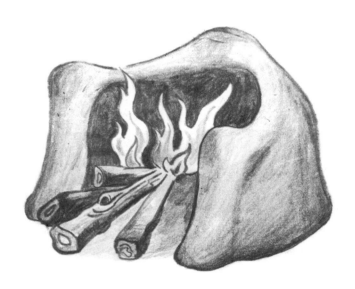

chulha

Baigan (Eggplant /Melongene) choka

This type of choka *is usually served with hot* sada roti *for break-fast at home. It is only now being sold at Indian food outlets in Trinidad.*

Ingredients
2 lbs /900 grms *baigan* (2, each weighing one pound)
4 cloves garlic
2 small onions
8 tsp /8 x 5 ml spoon vegetable oil
1 hot pepper (optional)
Salt to taste

Method
- Wash *baigan* and wipe dry.
- Rub skin with ½ teaspoon vegetable oil.
- Peel garlic cloves and leave whole.
- Make a small opening in each *baigan*, large enough to accommodate 2 cloves of garlic.
- Roast/grill on an open fire on a gas cooker or *chulha* (fireside).
- Keep turning with a *simthaa* (tongs) until all sides are roasted. (The *baigan* will become limp/tender when it is properly roasted).
- Cut *baigan* in halves lengthwise and scoop out pulp. Discard skin.
- Using a fork, crush garlic with roasted *baigan*.
- Heat oil and mix.
- Add salt, pepper and sauté *choka*
- Dice onions finely and add to *choka*.

Serves 3-4 persons.

Variations
In some parts of India, *dahi* (yogurt) and clove are added to the roasted *baigan* and served chilled.

31

Chataigne /Breadnut Talkari

This dish is traditionally served with hot parata roti *at large Indian dinners.*

Ingredients
2 green chataignes
2 dry coconuts (grated)
1/8 pt /75 mls vegetable oil
1 tsp / 1 x 5 ml spoon whole grain *geera* (cumin)
2 tsp 2 x 5 ml spoon ground *geera*
1 tsp / 1 x 5 ml spoon minced garlic
4 tsp /4 x 5 ml spoon curry powder
6 tsp /6 x 5 ml spoon minced garlic and *bandhaniya*
   (shado beni)
1 pot spoon / 50 mls water
2½ pts / 1500 mls water (for making coconut milk)
1 bundle chive (washed and finely chopped)
1 hot pepper
Salt to taste

Method
- Cut chataigne in halves, then cut each half in 4 pieces.
- Paste a little oil on hands.
- Peel off the outer skin.
- Remove the inner core deep enough so that the tip of the
  seeds are exposed.
- Separate seeds from pulp.
- Peel both the outer hard skin and the inner soft skin from
  the seeds.
- Cut pulp into small pieces.
- Wash chataigne and leave to drain in a collander.
- Prepare 2½ pints coconut milk from the grated coconut.
  (Mix well and strain milk from husk).

- Heat oil and add whole grain *geera*, 1 teaspoon garlic and chopped chive.
- Mix curry powder in 1 pot spoon water and add to pot.
- Stir in minced garlic and *bandhaniya*.
- Fry for 2 minutes and mix in chataigne so that chataigne is coated evenly with the curry.
- Add coconut milk and salt.
- Cook for 45 minutes.
- Add ground *geera*, mixing well into cooked chataigne .

Serves 6-8 persons.

simthaa

Curried Aloo

This dish is characteristic of Indo-Caribbean cuisine. This is the basic recipe for curried dishes, vegetarian as well as non-vegetarian.

Ingredients
2 lbs / 900 grms *aloo* (potato)
4 tsp / 4 x 5 ml spoon curry powder
6 tsp / 6 x 5 ml spoon water
1 pot spoon / 50 mls vegetable oil
4 tsp / 4 x 5 ml spoon minced garlic and *bandhaniya* (shado beni)
1 tsp / 1 x 5 ml ground *geera* (cumin)
2 pts / 1200 mls hot water
1 small onion diced finely
Hot pepper (optional)
Salt to taste

For Poran
1 tsp / 1 x 5 ml whole grain *geera*
1 tsp / 1 x 5 ml spoon crushed garlic

Method
•Peel, wash and cut *aloo* into small cubes about 1".
•Place in a dish with enough water to cover *aloo* and set aside.
•Heat oil in medium- sized iron pot.
•Add whole grain *geera* and crushed garlic to pot.
•Mix 6 teaspoons water with curry powder, onion and minced garlic and *bandhaniya* and add to pot.
•Fry/ sauté for about 2 minutes.
•Drain *aloo* and add to curry mixture in pot.
•Fry for another 2-3 minutes and add salt.
•Pour in hot water and stir.
•Cook until *aloo* is tender.
•Add ground *geera* and stir thoroughly.

1.Daahl 2.Goolgula 3.Kurma 4.Curried mango anchar
5.Fried caraillee

Vegetable market scene in the Caribbean.

Curried Mango

This is a very popular dish in the Caribbean East Indian cuisine. Both the sliced green mangoes from which the anchar *is made, and the* anchar *itself, can be stored in the refrigerator.*

Ingredients
6 half ripe mangoes (veer or long variety)
2 pot spoons /100 mls vegetable oil
4 tsp /4 x 5 ml spoon curry powder
¼ pt /150 mls water (to mix curry)
4 tsp /4 x 5 ml spoon minced garlic
3 pts / 1800 mls hot water
½ lb /225 grms brown sugar
1 tsp /1 x 5 ml spoon ground *geera* (cumin)
2 tsp / 2 x 5 ml spoon minced *bandhaniya* (shado beni)
1 hot pepper
Salt to taste

For *poran*
1 tsp / 1 x 5 ml spoon whole grain geera (cumin)
1 tsp /1 x 5 ml spoon minced garlic

Method
- Cut each mango lengthwise into half and then cut each half again into 4 lenghtwise pieces.
- Remove seeds, wash and put to drain.
- Heat oil in an iron pot.
- Add whole grain *geera* and 1 teaspoon garlic.
- Mix curry, *bandhaniya* and rest of garlic in 150 mls of water.
- Add curry to pot and let fry for 2 minutes.
- Add mango and mix up thoroughly so that mango slices are evenly coated with curry mixture.
- Add 3 pints hot water.
- Mix in salt, brown sugar and hot pepper.
- Add ground *geera* and mix thoroughly.

Serves 8-10 persons.

Curried Same/Seim

This dish is usually eaten for breakfast by Indians with any type of roti.

Ingredients
1½ lbs /675 grms same/seim.
8 tsp /8 x 5 mls spoon vegetable oil
2 pts /1200 mls water
8 tsp /8 x 5 ml spoon water
6 tsp /6 x 5 ml spoon curry powder
1 small head garlic (minced)
2 tsp /2 x 5 ml spoon ground *geera* (cumin)
2 small ripe tomatoes (cubed)
1 small onion (chopped)
4 large leaves minced *bandhaniya* (shado beni)
1 tsp /1 x 5 ml spoon whole grain *geera*
1 hot pepper
Salt to taste

Method
- Wash same and cut into small pieces about 1" long.
- Put 2 pints water to boil in a kettle.
- Heat oil in an iron pot.
- Add ½ teaspoon of crushed garlic and the whole grain *geera* to oil.
- Mix curry powder, minced *bandhaniya* and rest of garlic in 8 teaspoons water.
- Add curry mixture to oil and fry for 2 - 3 minutes.
- Mix in chopped onion and cubed tomatoes and fry for another ½ minute.
- Add same and stir so that the curry mixes in thoroughly.
- Add salt.
- Add boiling water and cook until tender.
- Stir in ground *geera.*

Serve with hot white rice or *roti*.

Serves 6-8 persons.

Variations
Potatoes can be added to this dish. Non-vegetarians can include salted fish or shrimp. If you are using salted fish, you would have to use little or no salt depending on the quantity of salted fish used.

iron pot

Flour Talkari

This dish looks and tastes like curried meat and is referred to as "curried goat." It was popular two generations ago.

Ingredients

1 lb / 450 grms white flour
1/3pt /200 mls water (to knead flour)
1 pot spoon / 50 mls vegetable oil
2 tsp / 2 x 5 ml spoon curry powder
8 tsp / 8 x 5 ml spoon water (to mix curry)
1 tsp / 1 x 5 ml spoon whole grain *geera* (cumin)
1 tsp / 1 x 5 ml spoon ground *geera*
4 tsp / 4 x 5 ml spoon minced garlic and *bandhaniya* (shado beni)
½ pt / 300 mls hot water
1 hot pepper (whole)
2 leaves podina
Salt to taste

Method

●Knead flour with water to make stiff dough.
●Wash dough under running water until you are left with the "gum-like" part of dough.
●Cut into small pieces ½" thick.
●Season with half of the minced garlic, *bandhaniya* and podina.
●Heat oil in iron pot and add whole grain *geera*.
●Mix curry powder with 8 teaspoons water and rest of garlic and *bandhaniya*.
●Add to pot and fry for 2-3 minutes.
●Add flour pieces and fry for 2-3 minutes more.
●Pour hot water and cook on a medium heat.
●Add salt and hot pepper.
●Mix in ground *geera* and stir thoroughly.

Serves 4-6 persons.

Fried bodi

This is a quick, easy - to - prepare dish which is traditionally served for breakfast and/or dinner. Nowadays, when one purchases a "vegetable roti," *bodi is one of the items served.*

Ingredients
1 lb /450 grms bodi
4 small ripe tomatoes
1 medium onion
4 tsp /4 x 5 ml spoon minced garlic
2 pot spoons /100 mls vegetable oil
Salt to taste
Hot pepper to taste (optional)

Method
•Wash bodi and cut/break into small pieces about 1" long.
(Remove threads at side if bodi is mature).
•Slice tomatoes thinly and dice onions very fine.
•Heat oil and fry onion, tomatoes and garlic for about 2 minutes.
•Add bodi, pepper and salt and stir.
•Cook for about 6-8 minutes, stirring occasionally.

Serves 4 persons.

Fried Caraillee / Bitter Cucumber

Non-vegetarians usually add salted fish to this dish. For vegetarians, it is equally delicious when eaten with daahl *and rice. Some people prefer to eat caraille half- cooked.*

Ingredients
2 lbs /900 grms caraillee/bitter cucumber
1 tsp /1 x 5 ml minced garlic
2 tsp /2 x 5 ml spoon salt..
Oil for frying

Method
• Slice caraillee lengthwise into halves.
• Scoop out pulp and seeds.
• Cut into very thin slices.
• Add salt, mix and leave to rest for about 1 hour.
• Squeeze all liquid from the caraillee to extract some of the bitter taste.
• Heat oil and add garlic.
• Fry caraillee until brown and crispy.

Serves 5-6 persons.

Variations
In south India, tamarind pulp, *hardi* (tumeric) and mustard seeds are added to make "fried karela."

Green Banana /"Fig" Talkari

This dish is prepared and eaten at home by Indo-Caribbean families; it is still not available at restaurants and Indian food outlets. It is rarely served at Indian functions.

Ingredients
2 lbs / 900 grms young green cooking "fig"/bananas
1 dry coconut (grated)
1 tsp /1 x 5 ml spoon whole grain *geera* (cumin)
1 tsp /1 x 5 ml spoon minced garlic
4 tsp /4 x 5 ml spoon minced garlic and freshly ground
   bandhaniya (shado beni)
4 tsp /4 x 5 ml spoon curry powder
1 tsp / 1 x 5 ml spoon ground *geera*
1 pot spoon /50 mls vegetable oil
2½ pts / 1500 mls water
6 tsp /6 x 5 ml spoon water (for curry powder)
Salt to taste
1 small onion (diced)
1 hot pepper

Method
•Peel green "figs" and cut into thin circular slices.
•Put into a dish with enough water to cover and set aside.
•Combine grated coconut with 2½ pints water.
•Strain coconut milk and discard husk.
•Heat oil in an iron pot.
•Add whole grain *geera* and 1 teaspoon garlic to hot oil.
•Mix in a small dish, curry powder, 6 teaspoons water
  minced garlic and *bandhaniya*.
•When garlic is brown, add curry mixture and sauté.
•Mix in onion, pepper and salt.
•Drain water from sliced green "fig."

- Add green "fig" to sauted curry mixture and fry for a few minutes, stirring occasionally.
- Add coconut milk and bring to the boil until green "fig" is tender.
- Mix in the ground *geera* and stir.

Serves 6 - 8 persons.

Variations
Non-vegetarians usually add salted fish to the "fig" *talkari* ingredients. This dish -- with or without meat/fish -- is unknown in Guyana. In India, ginger and *hardi* (tumeric) are used as additional ingredients, while coconut milk is not used at all.

Jhingee/Angled Loofah Talkari

This dish is rare in the Caribbean because the vine-creeper plant itself is hardly known, particularly by the younger generation of Indo-Caribbean people.

Ingredients
2 lbs / 900 grms *jhingee* (angled loofah)
4 tsp / 4 x 5 ml spoon vegetable oil
4 tsp / 4 x 5 ml spoon curry powder
4 large cloves garlic (minced)
6 leaves freshly ground *bandhaniya* (shado beni)
½ tsp / ½ of 5 ml spoon ground *geera* (cumin)
8 tsp / 8 x 5 ml spoon water

Method
●Peel and wash *jhingee.*
●Remove any seeds and cut into thin slices.
●Heat oil in small iron pot.
●Mix curry powder, minced garlic and *bandhaniya* in 8 teaspoons water.
●Add to pot and fry for about 2 minutes.
●Stir in *jhingee* making sure all pieces are coated evenly with curry mixture.
●Cover pot and cook on a slow heat for 12-15 minutes.
●When finished cooking, add *geera* and mix in thoroughly.

Serves 4-6 persons.

Variations
Non-vegetarians add finely chopped pieces of meat or salted fish when preparing this dish.

Kalounjee /Stuffed Bitter Gourd

This side dish is usually served with the main meal at most pujas
and other Hindu religious occasions.

Ingredients
1 lb /450 grms caraillee /bitter gourd /bitter cucumber /pomme
coolee
3 small pomme cytheres (peeled and grated)
3 cloves garlic
10 leaves fresh *bandhaniya* (shado beni)
2 tsp /2 x 5 ml spoon *anchar massala*
1 tsp /1 x 5 ml spoon ground *geera* (cumin)
6 tsp /6 x 5 ml spoon curry powder
1 pt /600 mls water
¼ lb /100 grms white flour
Salt to taste
Oil for deep frying
1 hot pepper

Method
•Cut caraillee crosswise into halves so that each half resembles
a cone and scoop out the inside pulp.
•Boil caraillee in 1 pint water with salt to taste for 5 minutes.
(Water should cover caraillee).
•Drain and allow to cool.
•Mince pepper, garlic and *bandhaniya.*
•Add this mixture to the grated pomme cythere.
•Mix in *anchar massala,* ground *geera,* curry powder and salt to
taste.
•Stuff mixture into caraillee cones.
•Paste the outsides of the caraillee using same mixture.
•Place on a floured surface and roll lightly.
•Deep fry in hot oil until golden brown.
•Drain on brown or absorbent paper.

Serves 6 persons.

Variations
The caraillee may be cut lengthways, but it must be tied with a thread to secure the filling. Grated green mango or tamarind may be substituted for pomme cythere. In India, this dish is called *bharwaan karele*. In Guyana, *kalounjee* is simmered in coconut milk after it has been fried.

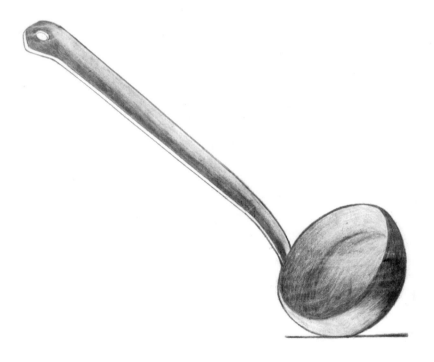

kalchul

Massala Caraillee

This dish is served particularly at the Hindu religious cere-monies of barahee *(12th day thanksgiving after the birth of a child) and* bandhara (13th day funeral rite).

Ingredients

1 lb / 450 grms caraillee / bitter gourd
3 green mangoes (verte/veer /long variety)
½ lb / 225 grms grated carrots
10 tsp / 10 x 5 spoon *anchar massala*
1 tsp / 1 x 5 ml spoon ground *geera* (cumin)
1/3 pt / 200 mls vegetable oil
1 head garlic (minced)
1 onion (finely chopped)
Salt to taste

Method

•Cut caraillee into halves crosswise and scoop out the inside.
•Cut into small pieces about 2" long and ¼ " thick.
•Peel mango and grate into small strips.
•Combine caraillee with the grated carrots and rest of ingred-ients (except vegetable oil).
•Heat oil and fry caraillee mixture for about 10-15 minutes, stirring occasionally.

Serves 6 persons.

1.Vegetable rice 2.Curhee 3.Gulab Jamoon 4.Mixed Bhaji

Traditional method of grinding spices, herbs and flavourings with a *sil* and *lorha*.

Lowkee / Bottle Gourd Talkari

The plant itself (Bottle gourd /<u>Lagenaria siceraria</u>) is hardly known by the younger generation of Indo-Caribbean people. In Trinidad it can be found in the country areas of Debe and Cunupia.

Ingredients
1 lowkee (about 2 lbs /900 grms)
4 tsp /4 x 5 ml spoon curry powder
4 tsp / 4 x 5 ml spoon minced garlic
2 tsp / 2 x 5 ml spoon minced *bandhaniya* (shado beni)
1 medium onion (chopped finely)
1 pot spoon / 50 mls vegetable oil
4 tsp / 4 x 5 ml spoon water (to mix curry)
1 tsp / 1 x 5 ml spoon ground *geera* (cumin)
1 hot pepper
Salt to taste

Method
•Peel lowkee and cut into quarters.
•Remove seeds and cut into small pieces.
•Wash and leave in some water.
•Heat oil, mix curry with water, onion, garlic and *bandhaniya* and fry for 2-3 minutes.
•Drain lowkee and add to pot.
•Turn it up properly and add salt and pepper.
•Stir well so that all pieces are completely coated with curry mixture.
•Add pepper and cook until soft, then add the *geera* and stir well.

Serves 4 persons.

Mixed Bhaji

This dish was traditionally served during the chatti *and* barahi *(6th and 12th day thanksgiving after the birth of a child) celebrations. Nowadays, it is served as a regular dish and is eaten even at Hindu religious ceremonies.*

Ingredients
1 bundle dasheen leaves (approx. 20 leaves)
4 ozs / 100 grms bodi
4 ozs / 100 grms caraillee / bitter gourd / pomme coolee
8 ozs / 225 grms *baigan* (melongene)
4-6 small ochroes
1 small head garlic (minced)
1 pot spoon / 50 mls vegetable oil
1 grated dry coconut
½ pt /300 mls water (for making coconut milk)
1 hot pepper
Salt to taste

Method
- Remove stems from dasheen leaves.
- Pick pointed tips of leaves and dispose.
- Wash thoroughly and cut dasheen leaves finely.
- Wash bodi and break /cut into small pieces about ¼" long.
- Peel and wash *baigan* and cut into thin slices about ¹/8" wide.
- Wash caraillee, cut and remove seeds.
- Cut into thin strips about 2" long and ¼" thick.
- Wash, dry and cut ochroes into thin slices about 1/8" thick.
- Heat oil and add 1 teaspoon minced garlic.
- Add rest of ingredients except the coconut.
- Combine grated coconut with ½ pint water.
- Strain coconut milk and discard husk.
- Add coconut milk to pot.

•Leave on medium heat until all vegetables are soft and all liquid has been absorbed.

Serves 4 - 6 persons.

Variations
Calorie-conscious persons use water instead of coconut milk. In some parts of India, tomatoes, *daah*l and ginger are added to the ingredients.

lota and tariya

Pumpkin talkari

All the varieties of pumpkin can be prepared in the same way and are equally tasty.

Ingredients
2 lbs/900 grms pumpkin
6 tsp/6 x 5 ml spoon vegetable oil
1 bundle chive (washed and finely chopped)
4 large cloves garlic (crushed)
1 tsp/ 1 x 5 ml spoon ground *geera* (cumin)
Salt to taste
Hot pepper to taste

Method
•Peel and wash pumpkin.
•Cut into small pieces/strips about 1" long.
•Heat oil in an iron pot and add garlic and chive
•Fry for a few seconds and then add pumpkin.
•Add salt and pepper and cook until pumpkin is soft.
•Using a *daahl ghotnee* (wooden swizzle stick), crush pumpkin until it is smooth and there are no whole pieces left.
•Add ground *geera* and stir thoroughly.

Serves 4-6 persons.

Variations
When pumpkin is young and without colour, it is ideal for currying. In Guyana, *massala* or curry powder is always added to the pot.

Serves 6 - 8 persons.

Saheena Talkari

This style of preparation makes the saheena *look and taste like curried fish. Some people refer to it as "vege-fish."*

Ingredients
1 doz *saheena* (see recipe for rolled-type)
4 tsp / 4 x 5 ml spoon curry powder
1 small onion (diced finely)
1 head garlic (minced)
6 leaves minced *bandhaniya* (shado beni)
2 pot spoons / 100 mls vegetable oil
1 tsp / 1 x 5 ml spoon ground *geera* (cumin)
6 tsp / 6 x 5 ml spoon water (to mix curry)
1 hot pepper
Salt to taste.

Method
• Heat oil in an iron pot.
• Meanwhile, mix curry powder, *bandhaniya* and garlic in 6 teaspoons water.
• Add onions to hot oil and fry for ½ minute; then stir in curry mixture.
• Allow to fry for about 2 minutes.
• Pour hot water and boil for a few minutes.
• Add *saheena* to pot.
• Cook for about 5-8 minutes depending on the thickness gravy required.
• Mix in *geera* and stir thoroughly.

Serves 8-10 persons.

Tomato Choka

This is a breakfast- dish which is eaten with sada roti. *It is believed to be tastier when the tomatoes are roasted on a* chulha *(fireside).*

Ingredients
1 lb /450 grms ripe red tomatoes
2 tsp / 2 x 5 ml spoon vegetable oil
1 small onion (diced)
2 cloves crushed garlic
1 hot pepper
Salt to taste

Method
●Wash tomatoes and wipe dry with a clean cloth.
●Put on an iron grid and roast on a gas cooker or a *chulha* (fireside) until charred.
●Allow to cool and remove skin.
●Using the end of the *belnaa* (rolling pin), pound tomatoes until pulpy.
●Mix in onion, salt and hot pepper.
●Heat oil in a *kalchul* (ladle) until piping hot and add garlic.
●Add to *choka*.
●Mix thoroughly.

Variations
The tomatoes can be boiled instead of roasted, using the same ingredients and method to make the *choka*.

Vegetable Rice

This is an original dish based on a traditional style of "vegetarian pelau"

Ingredients
1½ lbs / 675 grms brown rice
1 can / 450 grms pigeon peas (drained)
½ lb / 225 grms diced carrots
¼ lb / 100 grms diced sweet pepper
4 ozs / 100 grms bodi
4 ozs / 100 gms cauliflower
2 pot spoons / 100 mls vegetable oil
2 ozs / 50 grms brown sugar
1 head garlic (minced)
1 bundle chive (washed and finely chopped)
1 stalk celery (chopped finely)
1 grated dry coconut
5 pts / 3000 mls water (for making coconut milk)
1 hot pepper
Salt to taste

Method
•Prepare 5 pints coconut milk by mixing grated coconut and water and straining off husk..
•Heat oil in a large iron pot.
•Wash rice and drain.
•Add brown sugar to oil and "burn" until sugar turns brown-black and bubbly
•Add rice, stirring well until rice is thoroughly covered with browning.
•Mix in carrots, sweet pepper, bodi, cauliflower, garlic, chive and salt.
•Add coconut milk and hot pepper.
•Cook until rice is tender and then add pigeon peas.
•Mix in the celery and cover pot.

Serves 8-10 persons.

Making *loyahs* (balls) for *paratha roti* for a large Indian dinner.

Chutney aur Anchar (Chutneys and Pickles)

Amrak Anchar

This fruit (Amrak/Bilimbi/ <u>Averrhoa</u> <u>bilimbi</u>) *is hardly known by the younger generation of Indo-Caribbean people and the anchar is, therefore, rarely made. This type of pickle has a unique piquant flavour.*

Ingredients
2 lbs / 900 grms amrak /bilimbi
4 tsp / 4 x 5 ml spoon salt (to boil amrak)
1½ pts / 900 mls water
6 leaves *bandhaniya* (shado beni)
2 pot spoons / 100 mls vegetable oil
6 tsp / 6 x 5 ml spoon *anchar massala*
2 tsp / 2 x 5 ml spoon ground *geera* (cumin)
2 tsp / 2 x 5 ml spoon mustard oil
3 hot peppers
1 head minced garlic
Salt to taste

Method
•Boil amrak in 1½ pints water with 4 teaspoons salt.
•Wash hot peppers and add to amrak to boil.
•When amrak is soft drain in a collander.
•Heat oil in an iron pot.
•Mince garlic and *bandhaniya.*
•Fry /saute in oil for about 1minute.
•Add amrak, *anchar massala, geera* and salt to taste.
•Allow to cook for about 3-4 minutes.
•Add mustard oil and allow to cool.
•Bottle in a sterilised wide mouth jar.

Chalta / Elephant Apple Anchar

This type of anchar *appears regularly on kitchen tables when* chalta *is in season. It is said to liven up a meal, however insipid and bland.* Chalta anchar *is now sold by wayside vendors.*

Ingredients
3-4 young *chalta* (elephant apple) about 1½ lbs each
1/3 pt / 200 mls water
6 tsp / 6 x 5 ml spoon *anchar massala*
2 small heads minced garlic
2 tsp / 2 x 5 ml spoon ground *geera* (cumin)
1 tsp / 1 x 5 ml spoon mustard oil
¼ pt / 150 mls vegetable oil
3 hot peppers (optional)
Salt to taste

Method
•Cut *chalta* into thin slices about ¼" thick.
•Remove seed and wash.
•Bring 1/3 pint water to the boil.
•Add salt and cook *chalta* until tender.
•Drain *chalta* and transfer to large mixing bowl.
•Mince hot pepper and heat vegetable oil.
•Meanwhile, combine *chalta* with all remaining ingredients.
•Add hot oil and minced pepper and mix thoroughly.
•Store in sterilized open-mouth jar.

Coconut Chutney

This chutney *is often served when* daahl *is part of the menu. It is considered an appetizer. Any left-over* chutney *can be stored in the refrigerator for later use.*

Ingredients
1 medium dry coconut
3 large cloves garlic
5-6 large leaves *bandhaniya* (shado beni)
1 hot pepper
Salt to taste

Method
• Remove kernel from coconut shell.
• Wash, dry and roast on an open flame. (You can roast it over the flame in a stove using a fork).
• Scrape crust and wash.
• Grate finely.
• Using a *belnaa* (rolling pin) and *chowkee* (breadboard), grind kernel adding a few drops of water. (The water makes it easier to grind).
• Crush/mince garlic, pepper and *bandhaniya* together and add to coconut.
• Add salt.
• Mix thoroughly.

Serves 8 - 10 persons.

Variation
In India split black beans, chick peas, plain yogurt, tamarind, lime juice and ginger root are included in making *Gari ki chutni* (fresh coconut chutney). Coconut chutney is known as "coconut choka" in Guyana and is prepared in the same manner.

1. Grated pomme cythere chutney   2. Googanie
3. Kitchree   4. Fried bodi

Cover photo. 1. Mango anchar 2. Paratha roti 3. Chataigne **Talkari**
4. Pumpkin 5. **Channa** and **Aloo**

Grated Mango /Pomme cythere chutney

This type of chutney *is not as popular as the one that is cooked. The latter type takes a longer time to prepare. It is, nevertheless, equally tasty.*

Ingredients
2 half-ripe mangoes /pomme cytheres
4 medium- sized cloves of garlic
2 large leaves *bandhaniya* (shado beni)
1 tsp /1 x 5 ml spoon brown sugar
1 hot pepper
Salt to taste

Method
•Peel mangoes/ pomme cytheres, wash and grate.
•Mince garlic, pepper and *bandhan*iya.
•Add to grated mango /pomme cythere.
•Add salt and sugar and mix in thoroughly.

Serves 6 - 8 persons.

Variations
In India, vinegar, bay leaves, ginger and raisins are used with the green mangoes, which are sliced and put to boil until tender.

Lime Pepper Sauce

This type of pickle is made by many Indian families when peppers and limes are in abundance. It is bottled and sold at supermarkets and other food outlets.

Ingredients
1 doz ripe limes
8 - 10 hot peppers (minced)
4 heaped tsp / 4 x 5 ml heaped spoon ground *bandhaniya* (shado beni)
4 large finely grated onions
6 heaped tsp / 6 x 5 ml heaped spoon minced garlic
Salt to taste

Method
•Wash, cut and squeeze juice from limes. (Yield 150 mls.)
•Strain lime juice.
•Combine all ingredients and mix thoroughly.
•Store in sterilized wide-mouth jar and label.

Lasts longer when stored in a refrigerator

Variations
In India, sliced ginger and broken bay leaves are used as additional ingredients. The pickling jar is covered with a muslin cloth and left in the sun or in a warm place for 4 days.

Mango Anchar

Some people feel that an Indian menu is incomplete if it does not include mango anchar. *It is often prepared with additional peppers to give it a "hot" taste.*

Ingredients
10 half ripe mangoes
¼ pt /150 mls vegetable oil
1 tsp / 1 x 5 ml spoon whole grain *geera* (cumin)
½ lb / 225 grms brown sugar
4 tsp / 4 x 5 ml spoon minced garlic
4 tsp / 4 x 5 ml spoon ground *geera*
8 tsp /8 x 5 ml spoon *anchar massala*
1 hot pepper (optional)
Salt to taste
Water (to boil/steam mango)

Method
•Cut mangoes (with skin) lenghtwise into halves and then cut each half into 4 pieces.
•Put water to boil in a large iron pot.
•Wash mango pieces and remove seed.
•Add mango to boiling water. (Water should cover mango).
•Add salt and pepper. (Leave pepper whole).
•When mango is soft, remove pepper and set aside.
•Strain mango in a large collander.
•Put oil to hot in the same iron pot.
•Add whole grain *geera* and allow to get brown.
•Add garlic and fry for ½ minute.
•Add mango to pot.
•Mix in brown sugar, ground *geera, anchar massala* and pepper.
•Allow to fry for a few minutes more.

•Store in sterilized wide-mouth jar and label.

Variations
The amount of sugar to be added would depend on the degree of greenness of the mango and one's preference for taste. In India, *hardi* (tumeric), *hing* (asafoetida) and mustard seed are used as ingredients.

okhree and musar

Mango Chutney

Mango chutney *is used as the Indian counterpart to American pickles; it is eaten as a condiment with* aloo pie, saheena *and* kachowrie, *and is always served with* phulowrie.

Ingredients
3 half-ripe large mangoes
12 tsp /12 x 5 ml spoons brown sugar
6 large leaves *bandhaniya* (shado beni)
1 tsp /1 x 5 ml spoon *hardi* (tumeric)
3 pts /1800 mls water
2 tsp /2 x 5 ml spoon ground *geera* (cumin)
1 medium sized head garlic minced
1 hot pepper (optional)
Salt to taste

Method
- Cut mangoes into halves (lengthwise) and then cut each half into 6-8 pieces (about 1" long).
- Put water to boil.
- Wash mangoes and add to boiling water.
- Add pepper.
- Mix in *hardi*, crushed garlic, sugar, salt and *bandhaniya*.
- When mango is soft, swizzle mixture with a *daahl ghotnee* (wooden swizzle stick).
- Add ground *geera* and mix in properly.

Serves 12-15 persons.

Variations
In India finely grated coconut, ginger and *dahi* (yogurt) are fried with the chopped mango to make *aam chatni* (mango chutney). Some cooks grind the ingredients with mint on a *sil* and *lorha* (grinding stones) and serve it chiledl as a side dish. In Jamaica, however, tamarind and vinegar are boiled with the main ingredients.

Mango Kuchilla

Grated or shredded pickles of this kind are common in many Indo-Caribbean kitchens. They are only now being bottled and sold at the supermarkets. Non-Indians are now acquiring a taste for kuchilla.

Ingredients
8 young green mangoes
4 pot spoons /200 mls vegetable oil
6 tsp / 6 x 5 ml spoon *anchar massala*
2 tsp / 2 x 5 ml spoon ground *geera* (cumin)
2 large heads garlic
4 tsp / 4 x 5 ml spoon mustard oil
8 tsp /8 x 5 ml spoon vinegar
2 tsp / 2 x 5 ml spoon brown sugar
2 hot peppers (optional)
Salt to taste

Method
•Wash mangoes and grate into fine strips. (Peel the mangoes if you wish).
•Using a fine cloth, squeeze out liquid and discard.
•Spread shredded mango on a clean cloth on a flat surface to dry in the sun.
•Allow to dry for about 2-3 hours, turning mango every ½ hour.
•Heat oil in a saucepan.
•Combine mango and hot oil in a large mixing bowl.
•Mince garlic and pepper with vinegar.
•Add mixture to mango.
•Stir in *geera, anchar massala* and sugar and mix.
•Add mustard oil and salt and mix all ingredients thoroughly.
•Allow to cool.
•Bottle *kuchilla* in sterilised wide-mouth glass jar.

Variations

The amount of sugar to be added would depend on the degree of greenness of the mangoes. The ideal mango to be chosen to make *kuchilla* is one that has a lot of pulp. In Guyana, the liquid from the green mango is not extracted and the mixture is fried in oil.

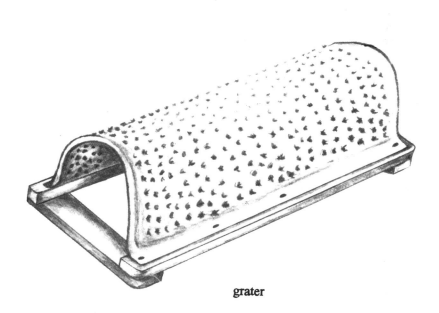

grater

Pepper Chutney

This type of chutney *is rarely served nowadays. It is, however, still homemade and eaten mainly by rural Indians as an appetizer.*

Ingredients
3 hot peppers
2 large cloves garlic
6 large fresh leaves *bandhaniya* (shado beni)
4 tsp/4 x 5 ml spoon vegetable oil (to *chownkay*)
Salt to taste

Method
• Roast pepper and garlic on an open fire (*chulha* or gas cooker).
• Pound pepper and garlic together.
• Mince *bandhaniya* and add to mixture.
• Heat oil in a *kalchul* (ladle).
• Add piping hot oil and salt to mixture and work in well.

Variation
In Guyana, all the ingredients are minced and then fried with mustard oil.

Tamarind Chutney

This sour/sweet relish is often served with snacks like saheena, phulowrie, aloo *pie and* kachowrie. *It may be used with any kind of food to enhance the food's flavour.*

Ingredients
6-8 ozs shelled ripe tamarind
4 tsp / 4 x 5 ml spoon minced garlic and *bandhaniya* (shado beni)
6 tsp / 6 x 5 ml spoon brown sugar
1/6 pt / 100 mls water
Water for sauce (about 150-200 mls)
1 hot pepper (minced)
Pinch of ground *geera* (cumin)
Salt to taste.

Method
•Rinse tamarind lightly in a bowl of water.
•Add 150-200 mls water to make a thick sauce.
•Leave to soak for 10-15 minutes.
•Mash with fingers until pulp separates from seeds.
•Mix rest of ingredients with tamarind except the pepper.
•Using a spoon, add pepper and mix thoroughly.

Variations
In India, raw cane sugar is substituted for brown sugar and freshly ground black pepper, finely chopped fresh ginger root and fresh lemon juice are used as additional ingredients.

Guyanese man cooking in a yard for a large Indian feast.
The stove is made from an oil drum fueled by firewood.

Namkeen aur Chat (Snacks)

Aloo Pie

Aloo *pie is indigenous to the Caribbean. It is sold at Indian delicacy outlets and by wayside vendors and is eaten with any kind of* chutney.

Ingredients
½ lb / 225 grms sifted white flour
1 tsp / 1 x 5 ml spoon baking powder
¼ - 1/3 pt / 150 - 200 mls water
1 tsp / 1 x 5 ml spoon vegetable oil
Vegetable oil for frying
Pinch salt

Filling
3/4 lb /350 grms potatoes
2 tsp / 2 x 5 ml spoon ground *geera* (cumin)
1 small diced onion
2 cloves minced garlic
1 minced hot pepper
Water to boil potatoes
Salt to taste

Method
•Knead flour with salt and baking powder using water.
•Paste dough with 1 teaspoon vegetable oil.
•Cover and leave to rest for 20-30 minutes.
•Boil potatoes until tender (water should cover potato).
•Mash thoroughly and add all other ingredients.
•Make 6 small *loyahs* with dough; leave to rest for 10 minutes.
•Roll *loyah* on floured surface 6" in diameter.
•Place 2 tablespoons filling in centre of circle and fold into a half moon.
•Seal edges by damping with water and pinching together.
•Heat oil and fry until golden brown taking care not to crowd the pot.

Baiganee

Baiganee *is made on special Hindu religious and other occasions. It is frequently found at Indian delicacy outlets and is usually eaten with some kind of* chutney

Ingredients

1 lb/450 grms *baigan* (eggplant)
8 ozs /225 grms ground *daahl* (split peas)
½ tsp / ½ of 5 ml spoon *hardi* (tumeric)
3 large leaves minced *bandhaniya* (shado beni)
¾ heaped tsp / ¾ of 5 ml spoon baking powder
3 large cloves garlic (crushed)
½ tsp / ½ of 5 ml spoon ground *geera* (cumin)
¼ pt /150 mls water
3 ozs /75 grms sifted white flour
Salt to taste
Oil for deep frying

Method

- Combine *daahl* and flour in a large mixing bowl.
- Add *hardi*, baking powder and garlic.
- Mix in *bandhaniya, geera* and salt.
- Add water and mix to make a soft dough.
- Wash and cut *baigan* into round slices about ½ cm thick.
- Heat oil.
- Paste eggplant slices on both sides with *daahl* mixture, wetting hands occasionally in a small bowl of water.
- Fry until golden brown and crisp.
- Drain on brown paper.

Makes 2 dozens.

Variations

In India, *ghee* (clarified butter) is used for deep frying instead of the oil. In Guyana, pieces of boiled cassava are added to the mixture.

Doubles

Doubles (a chick pea/ channa *sandwich made with* bara) *is indigenous to Trinidad. It is sold by numerous wayside vendors who serve it with* chutney, kuchilla *or pepper. In North America, where it is now being sold, it is referred to as "channa burger."*

Ingredients
½ lb / 225 grms white flour
1 tsp / 1 x 5 ml spoon instant yeast
1 tsp / 1 x 5 ml spoon *hardi* (tumeric) powder
1 tsp / 1 x 5 ml spoon ground *geera* (cumin)
$^1/6$ pt / 100 mls water
Oil for frying
Salt to taste

Filling
½ lb / 225 grms *channa* (chick peas)
4 tsp / 4 x 5 ml spoon curry powder
4 cloves minced garlic
1 small onion (finely diced)
1 pot spoon / 50 mls water
1 pot spoon /50 mls vegetable oil
½ tsp / ½ of 5 ml spoon ground *geera*
2 pints / 1200 mls water (to soak *channa*)
2 litres /2000 mls hot water (to boil *channa*)
6 leaves minced *bandhaniya* (shado beni)
4 karapulé leaves
1 hot pepper
Salt to taste

Method

•**Method for *bara*.**
•Combine flour with salt, yeast, *hardi* and *geera*.
•Mix thoroughly and add water to make a soft dough.
•Leave to rise for about 2 hours.
•Heat oil to fry *bara*.
•Moisten hands with water and take about 2 tablespoons of dough in hand and flatten into a circle about 4" in diameter.
•Fry on medium heat until light brown in colour.
•Drain on brown or absorbent paper.

•**Method for *channa* filling**
•Pre soak *channa* overnight and boil with salt in 2 pints water until tender.
•Drain *channa* .
•Heat oil until piping hot.
•Mix garlic, onion, curry powder, *bandhaniya,* karapulé and hot pepper in 50 mls water.
•Fry / sauté for 2-3 minutes.
•Add *channa* to pot and stir thoroughly.
•Add more water to cook if *channa* is not tender.
•Mix in ground *geera*, stir and set aside.

Makes 1 dozen *bara*.

Serve with mango *chutney* or pepper sauce.

Kachowrie

Kachowrie *is sold at Indian food outlets in Trinidad and is eaten as a snack with any kind of* chutney.

Ingredients

8 ozs / 225 grms ground *daahl* (split peas) or ground *channa* (chick peas)
4 ozs / 100 grms sifted white flour
4 ozs / 100 grms *aloo* (potato)
2 tsp / 2 x 5 ml spoon baking powder
1 tsp / 1 x 5 ml spoon ground *geera* (cumin)
2 tsp / 2 x 5 ml spoon garlic
2 tsp / 2 x 5 ml spoon *bandhaniya* (shado beni)
1 tsp / 1 x 5 ml spoon *hardi* (tumeric) powder
¾ pt / 450 mls vegetable oil (for frying)
½ pt / 300 mls water
Salt to taste

Method

- Mix ground *daahl / channa* with all the dry ingredients.
- Mince garlic and *bandhaniya* and add to mixture.
- Make a soft dough with water.
- Peel, wash and grate *aloo* into fine strips (like carrots) and add to dough.
- Heat oil in iron pot until piping hot.
- Make dough into balls (the size of a golf ball).
- Using wet fingers, flatten out ½" thick between the palms of hands.
- Fry on both sides until golden brown.

Makes 1½ dozen.

Serve with chutney.

1.Aloo pie 2.Kachowrie 3.Phulowrie 4.Saheena 5.Mango Chutney 6.Baiganie

Wayside "doubles" vendor. "Doubles" is indigenous to Trinidad.

Phulowrie

Phulowrie *is eaten as a snack with any type of* chutney. *It is easily available at* roti *shops and other Indian food outlets.* Phulowrie *is used in the making of* curhee.

Ingredients
½ lb / 225 grms ground *daahl* (split peas)
¼ lb /100 grms sifted white flour
½ tsp / ½ of 5 ml spoon *hardi* (tumeric)
¾ tsp / ¾ of 5 ml spoon baking powder
½ tsp / ½ of 5 ml spoon of ground *geera* (cumin)
½ pt / 300 mls vegetable oil
¼ pt /150 mls water (to make dough)
2 cloves garlic (minced)

Method
•Sift ground *daahl* and flour in a large mixing bowl.
•Combine with baking powder, *hardi* and *geera*.
•Mix in garlic.
•Add water to make a soft dough.
•Heat oil in a round - bottom iron pot.
•Drop mixture by tablespoons into hot oil and fry over a medium heat until golden brown.
•Drain on brown or absorbent paper.

Serve hot with tamarind *chutney*.

Makes 3 dozens.

Saheena

This is a popular style of preparing saheena *which is sold at many Indian food outlets in Trinidad . In Guyana,* saheena *is hardly known.*

Ingredients
1 lb / 450 grms ground *daahl* (split peas)
1 doz large dasheen leaves
4 tsp / 4 x 5 ml spoon minced garlic
½ tsp / ½ of 5 ml spoon *hardi* (tumeric)
2 tsp / 2 x 5 ml spoon ground *geera* (cumin)
4 tsp / 4 x 5 ml spoon baking powder
1 pt / 600 mls water (to blanche leaves)
¼ pt / 150 mls water
½ litre /500 mls vegetable oil (for frying)
Salt to taste

Method
•Bring to boil 1 pint water.
•Remove stems from dasheen leaves and pick pointed tips of leaves and dispose.
•Using a fork, dip each leaf in boiling water for just a few seconds.
•Allow leaves to cool.
•Combine ground *daahl,* hardi, salt, garlic, *geera* and baking powder in a fairly large mixing bowl.
•Add ¼ pint water to make a soft batter.
•Spread a dasheen leaf with the darker side facing down on a flat clean surface or pastry board.
•Using hands, paste thinly some of the batter on leaf.
•Spread a second leaf over paste and again paste thinly with batter.
•Repeat procedure until you have used 6 leaves.
•Roll tightly (like a Swiss roll) and tuck in edges.

- Use remaining 6 leaves and make another roll.
- Heat oil in an iron pot.
- Using a very sharp knife, cut *saheena* roll into thin slices about ½" thick.
- Paste some batter on both sides and fry on medium heat until golden brown.

Makes 1½ dozens.

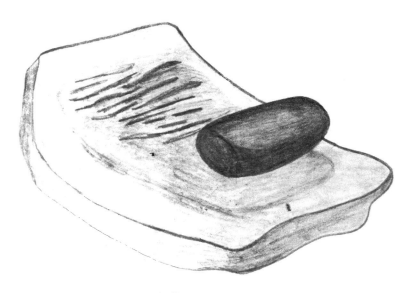

sil and lorhaa

Saheena (Short-cut method)

This is eaten as a snack with any type of chutney. *It is usually sold at* roti *shops and other Indian delicacy outlets.*

Ingredients
½ lb /225 grms white flour
1 doz medium sized dasheen leaves
2 heaped tsp /2 x 5 ml spoon baking powder
5 large cloves garlic
1 tsp /1 x 5 ml spoon ground *geera* (cumin)
½ lb /225 grms ground *daahl* (split peas)
1 tsp /1 x 5 ml spoon *hardi* (tumeric) powder
1 /3 pt / 200 mls water
6 large leaves *bandhaniya* (shado beni)
1 lime
Oil for deep frying
Salt to taste

Method
- Combine flour, *daahl* and salt in a large mixing bowl.
- Separate dasheen leaves from stem.
- Pick pointed tips of the leaves and dispose.
- Dip each leaf in boiling water for about one minute.
- Allow to cool.
- Chip dasheen leaves finely and add juice of lime.
- Add to flour mixture.
- Add rest of the ingredients and mix evenly.
- Mix in water to make a soft batter.
- Heat oil.
- Make small balls with the batter and flatten each ball using the palm of your hand. (It should resemble a pattie).
- Fry over medium heat until golden brown.

Makes about 1-1½ dozens.

Serve with mango or tamarind *chutney*.

Methai (Sweets and Desserts)

Barfee

Barfee *is usually offered as part of the* parsad *(oblation) during Hindu ceremonial worship. It is always square-shaped and is now being sold at Indian food outlets as an item in their sweetmeat menu.*

Ingredients
1 lb / 450 grms powdered milk
¾ lb / 350 grms granulated sugar
¾ pt / 450 mls water
1 tin milk cream
1 tsp / 1 x 5 ml spoon ground *elychee* (cardamom)
1 tsp / 1 x 5 ml spoon almond essence
2 ozs / 50 grms fresh ginger
Cake decorations (coloured sprinkles)
Few drops of rose water
Pat of butter

Method
• Mix powdered milk and cream until well blended.
• Pass through a sieve or "sifter".
• Add *elychee* and ginger and mix well.
• Boil sugar and water, adding rose water and almond essence.
• Allow sugar mixture to form a light syrup.
• Add to milk mixture.
• Grease a flat square dish with butter and pour mixture in.
• Using a spatula or back of spoon, spread mixture evenly.
• Sprinkle with cake decorations.
• When cool, cut into 1" squares and space out with a spatula to dry.

Makes 2 dozen

Batasa

This sweetmeat is served as part of the parsad *(oblation) during Hindu ceremonial worship.*

Ingredients
½ pt / 300 mls water
½ lb / 225 grms granulated sugar

Method
●Put water to boil.
●Add sugar and boil until syrup spins a thread.
●Pour spoon fulls (pot spoon) on a banana leaf and leave to crystalize.

Makes 4-6 batasa.

Dahee (Yogurt)

Generally Indians of the Caribbean use dahee as a dessert. Traditionally, dahee was used in cooking and in marinades or as an accompaniment to salads.

Ingredients
1 pt / 600 mls fresh cow's milk
1 pot spoon / 50 mls commercial, unflavoured *dahee* (yogurt)

Method
•Boil milk on low heat for about 1 hour.
•Allow to cool (until luke warm).
•Mix in yogurt thoroughly with boiled milk.
•Cover and leave in a warm place until it sets. (This process takes 10-12 hours).
•Refrigerate *dahee.*
•Sweeten with brown sugar.
•Serve chilled.

Serves 3-4 persons.

Variations
In India, raw cane sugar, crushed *hardi* (tumeric), rose water, chopped nuts, ground cinnamon and cardamom are whisked thoroughly in the mixture. The yogurt used in many dishes is squeezed through a fine woven cloth or napkin to expel surplus moisture. In the Caribbean, a few drops of lime is added to accelerate the setting process and also to preserve the *dahee.*

Eggless Cake

This cake is prepared especially for vegetarians.

Ingredients
1 lb / 450 grms sifted white flour
1 lb / 450 grms granulated sugar
1 lb / 450 grms butter or margarine
2 packs / 500 mls evaporated milk
4 tsp / 4 x 5 ml spoon baking powder
6 tsp / 6 x 5 ml spoon almond or vanilla essence
2 tsp /2 x 5 ml spoon ground cinnamon

Method
•Cream butter and sugar, pouring in milk a little at a time until mixture is smooth and fluffy.
•Add baking-powder to flour.
•Fold in flour a little at a time.
•Add rest of ingredients.
•Grease two 8" baking tins with a little butter and sprinkle lightly with flour.
•Divide mixture into 2 equal parts and pour into baking tins.
•Bake for 45 minutes at 350° F or regulo 4.

Cool well on rack.

Goolgula

This dish is not very popular nowadays. It is becoming less known to the younger generation of Indo-Caribbean people.

Ingredients
1 lb /450 grms ripe bananas (sucrier/seekea variety)
1 lb /450 grms white flour
8 tsp / 8 x 5 ml spoon brown sugar
¼ tsp / ¼ of 5 ml spoon spice
1 tsp / 1 x 5 ml spoon *elychee* (cardamom)
2 ozs /50 grms raisins or currants.
1 tsp / 1 x 5 ml spoon baking powder
½ pt /300 mls water
A few drops of mixed essence
Oil for deep frying

Method
- Wash, peel and mash bananas.
- Sift flour into a large mixing bowl.
- Combine flour with sugar, cinnamon, *elychee*, baking powder and raisins.
- Mix in mashed bananas.
- Add enough water to make a soft dough.
- Add essence.
- Heat oil.
- Form dough into small balls and fry until golden brown.

Makes 3 dozen

Variations
In some parts of India, vanilla and grated nutmeg are added to the ingredients. In Jamaica, margarine from the refrigerator is sliced and substituted for the ripe bananas.

Gulab Jamoon

This sweetmeat is served at Hindu religious ceremonies as a dessert. It can be found otherwise at Indian delicacy outlets.

Ingredients
1½ lbs / 675 grms white flour
¾ lb / 350 grms butter
1 lb / 450 grms powdered milk
½ tin / 198 grms condensed milk
1/3 pt / 200 mls evaporated milk
1/3 pt / 200 mls water
2 tsp / 2 x 5 ml spoon *elychee* (cardamom)
1 tsp / 1 x 5 ml spoon ground cinnamon
3 tsp / 3 x 5 ml spoon freshly ground ginger
Vegetable oil for frying

For phaag (syrup)
1½ lbs / 675 mls granulated sugar
2 pts / 1200 mls water

Method
●Combine flour and powdered milk in a large bowl.
●Rub in butter into flour mixture with fingers until it looks   like fine bread crumbs.
●Mix in *elychee,* cinnamon and ginger.
●Add condensed milk, evaporated milk and water, and mix to a stiff dough.
●Cover and leave for about 30-45 minutes.
●Heat oil in an iron pot.
●Break dough into small pieces and form into almond shapes. about 2-3" in length and 2½ -3" in thickness.
●Fry over low heat until golden brown using a slotted spoon.
●Remove from oil and drain on absorbent paper.
●Place in a deep dish.

- Boil sugar and water until it forms a syrup.
- Pour syrup over *gulab jamoon* and keep turning until syrup crystallizes and becomes hard. (Turn gently to prevent *gulab jamoon* from breaking up).

Makes 7 dozens.

Variations
Some cooks use *ghee* (clarified butter) for frying and as a substitute for the butter in making the dough. The soft dough is sometimes divided and made into balls instead of almond shapes.

jharnaa

1.Pera 2.Ladoo 3.Jalebi

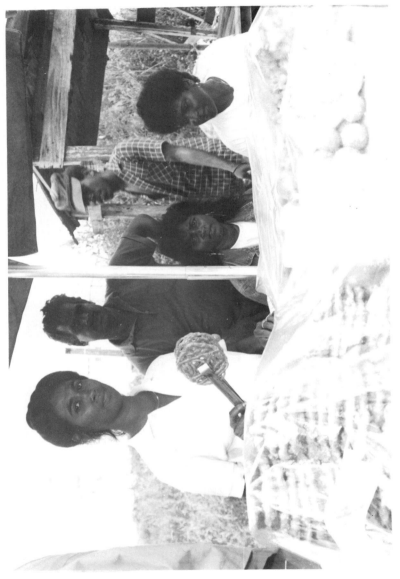

Typical Indian sweetmeat stall in Trinidad. From left, jalebi, pera, ladoo and kurma.

Halwa / Hulwa

This dish is prepared and eaten only during the chhati *and* barahi *(6th and 12th day thanksgiving for the birth of a child) celebrations. It is offered first by the mother of the child to the respective diety and then served to the guests at the ceremony.*

Ingredients
8 ozs / 225 grms sifted white flour
8 ozs / 225 grms granulated sugar
1 oz / 25 grms halwa / hulwa *massala*
2 ozs / 50 grms freshly grated ginger
½ tsp / ½ of 5 ml spoon whole grain *geera* (cumin)
½ pt / 300 mls evaporated milk
1 1/6 pt / 700 mls water
1/6 pt / 100 mls water (to mix *massala*)
1½ ozs / 38 grms *ghee* (clarified butter)

Method
•Parch flour in an iron pot on medium heat for about 5-6 minutes.
•Allow to cool and sift into a fairly large mixing bowl.
•Mix flour with ground ginger and sugar.
•Add milk and 1 1/6 pints water to flour and, using hands, stir until mixture is smooth.
•Heat ghee and add *geera.*
•Mix *halwa massala* in 100 mls water.
•Add to pot and fry for about 10 minutes on a very slow heat, stirring pot constantly.
•Stir flour mixture and add to pot.
•Keep turning until all the liquid has been absorbed.

Serve with *dosti roti* or as a side dish.

Serves 10-12 persons

Halwa massala preparation

If you are making your own *halwa massala*, you have to combine *massala, hardi* (tumeric), ginger and *jawine* and grind on a *sil*.

If you are using the prepared *halwa massala* from the *puja* shop, you should follow instructions given on the label.

belnaa and chowkee

Jalebi

Jalebi *(sweet coils in syrup) piled in stacks adds colour to a table laid with sweetmeat.*

Ingredients
½ lb / 225 grms white flour
½ pt / 300 mls warm water
1 pot spoon / 50 mls unflavoured *dahee* (yogurt)
Few drops of yellow food colour
Oil or *ghee* for deep frying

For Syrup
½ pt / 300 mls water
½ lb / 225 grms sugar
1 tsp / 1 x 5 ml spoon *elychee* (cardamom)

Method
•Mix flour, *dahee* and warm water together to make a smooth batter.
•Add 2 - 3 drops yellow food colour.
•Cover with a clean cloth and leave to stand overnight.
•Boil sugar, water and *elychee* to make thick syrup.
•Heat *ghee* or oil in an iron pot.
•Pour batter through a pastry bag or narrow funnel, into hot oil using a circular motion to form coils about 4" in diameter.
•Cook until light brown and drain with a slotted spoon.
•Dip *jalebis* in hot syrup and let syrup run through thoroughly. (Do not allow to get soft).
•Place on a stack to stand.

Makes 1 dozen.

Variations
In India, yeast is combined with the warm water and flour and beaten with a small *dabla* (wooden spoon) until mixture is very smooth.

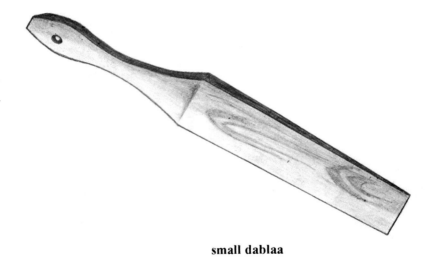

small dablaa

Kurma (1)

This sweetmeat is well-liked by non-Indians in the Caribbean and is available in snacks packs at most food stores in Trinidad. It is served mainly at Indian weddings and is referred to as "meetai" in Guyana.

Ingredients

5 lbs / 2250 grms sifted white flour
1 lb / 450 grms butter or margarine
1 tin / 397 grms condensed milk
½ pt / 300 mls evaporated milk
¹/3 pt / 200 mls water
4 ozs / 100 grms freshly grated ginger
3 tsp / 3 x 5 ml spoon ground *elychee* (cardamom)
2 tsp / 2 x 5 ml spoon ground cinnamon
Vegetable oil for frying

For *Phaag* (Syrup)

¼ litre / 250 mls water
1½ lb / 675 grms granulated sugar

Method

• Rub butter into flour until it looks like fine bread crumbs.
• Mix in remaining dry ingredients.
• Add all other ingredients, to make a soft dough.
• Leave to rest for 5-10 minutes.
• Divide dough into 5 equal parts and make 5 *loyahs* (balls)
• Heat oil in iron pot over medium flame.
• Roll out *loyahs* about ½" thick.
• Cut into strips about 1" wide.
• Roll each strip between palms of the hands until round like a pencil.
• Cut strips into small pieces about ¾" long.
• Fry until golden brown.

•Drain on brown or absorbent paper and put in a large bowl.
•Boil water and sugar until it forms a syrup.
•Pour on *kurma* and turn briskly until the sugar crystalizes.

Makes about 150 *kurmas*.

goglet

Kurma (11)

This is the type of kurma *that is found at commercial outlets and is longer and thinner than kurma (1).*

Ingredients
½ lb / 225 grms white flour
¼ pt / 150 mls water
1 small grated coconut
Oil for deep frying

For Syrup
½ lb / 225 grms granulated sugar
1/3 pt / 200 mls water
1 stick cinnamon

Method
●Mix ¼ pint water with grated coconut.
●Strain off liquid and discard husk.
●Knead flour with coconut milk to form a stiff dough.
●Divide into 2 equals portions to make 2 *loyahs* (balls).
●Roll out on a flat floured surface ¼" thick and cut into strips 2" long.
●Heat oil and fry until golden brown.
●Drain on brown paper and put in a deep metal bowl.
●Boil sugar and water and cinnamon until syrup spins a thread.
●Pour on *kurma* and turn briskly until syrup crystallizes.

Makes 6 dozen.

Ladoo

This is a popular sweetmeat which can be found at Indian delicacy outlets in the Caribbean.

Ingredients

½ lb / 225 grms ground *daahl* (split peas)
1/3 pint / 200 mls water
¼ tin / 100 grms condensed milk
6 ozs / 450 grms granulated sugar
2 tsp / 2 x 5 ml spoon freshly ground ginger
2 tsp / 2 x 5 ml spoon ground *elychee* (cardamom)
1 oz / 25 grms *ghee* (clarified butter)
½ pt /300 mls water
Oil for deep frying

Method

•Mix *daahl* with ¾ pint water.
•Heat oil.
•Pass *daahl* mixture through a *jharnaa* (a type of slotted spoon) and let fall in tiny strips into hot oil.
•Fry until light brown and drain on brown paper.
•Grind in a hand mill.
•Boil ½ pint water and sugar until syrup spins a thread.
•Add condensed milk, *ghee,* ginger and *elychee* to *daahl* mixture.
•Mix in syrup and shape into small balls while still hot.

Makes 1 dozen.

Lupsee

This dish is prepared specifically for Durga puja *(Hindu ceremonial worship in praise of an aspect of the Divine Mother). It is served with* sohari *(resembles a small fried pancake) as part of the* parsad *(oblation) and is also eaten as a dessert.*

Ingredients
8 ozs / 225 grms white flour
½ pt /300 mls evaporated milk
8 ozs / 225 grms granulated sugar
2 ozs / 50 grms *ghee* (clarified butter)
2 ozs / 50 grms raisins
1 pt / 600 mls water

Method
•Sift flour and parch for about 5 minutes on slow heat.
•Allow to cool and sift again.
•Heat *ghee* in an iron pot.
•Meanwhile, mix flour with rest of ingredients, adding dry ingredients first and then liquid.
•Add mixture to pot and lower heat.
•Cook until liquid has been absorbed.

Serves 6-8 persons.

Maleeda

Maleeda *is made as an oblation for Hosay (Shia Muslim com-
memoration of the death of Hassan and Husain, grandsons of
the Prophet Muhammed) and for all Islamic ceremonies.*

Ingredients
2 *paratha roti* (see recipe for *paratha roti)*
4 oz /100 grms granulated sugar.
1 oz /25 grms butter or margarine
10 tsp / 10 x 5 ml spoon condensed milk
½ tsp / ½ of 5 ml spoon black pepper
1 tsp / 1 x 5 ml spoon ground cinnamon
2 tsp / 2 x 5 ml spoon *elychee* (cardamom)
4 ozs / 100 grms raisins
2 tsp / 2 x 5 ml spoon almond essence
Diced cherries (optional)
Nuts (optional)

Method
• Wrap hot *paratha* in a clean cloth.
• Pound   with handle of *belnaa* until it crumbles into small
  pieces.
• Empty *roti* shreds into a large mixing bowl.
• Add sugar, black pepper, cinnamon, cardamom, raisins, nuts
  and cherries.
• Mix thoroughly.
• Mix in the rest of ingredients thoroughly and make into small
  balls.

Makes 12.

Panjaree

This is sprinkled on the parsad *(oblation) and is served only during* pujas *(Hindu ceremonial worship). It was more popular in the Caribbean before the 1960s.*

Ingredients
1 lb / 450 grms white rice
6 ozs / 175 grms granulated sugar
2 ozs / 50 grms *ghee* (clarified butter)
2 tsp / 2 x 5 ml spoon black pepper

Method
•Pick, wash and put rice to dry on a clean cloth in the sun.
•Grind rice very fine using a handmill.
•Heat *ghee* in an iron pot.
•Add ground white rice to pot and lower heat.
•Keep turning for about 7-8 minutes.
•Remove ground rice from pot and allow to cool.
• Mix in sugar and black pepper.

Makes approx. 1½ lbs.

Variations
In Guyana, parched flour is sometimes substituted for the ground white rice.

Parsad (Prasad / Mohan Bhog)

Parsad *is the sacred food offering distributed to guests before the main meal at all* pujas *(Hindu ceremonial worship). It is an oblation, and refusal to accept it by anyone is considered an insult to God.*

Ingredients
2½ lbs /1125 grms sifted white flour
2½ lbs /1125 grms *ghee* (clarified butter)
¼ lb /100 grms *munaka* (raisins or currants)
1 pk (14 ozs/350 grms) cream of wheat
2 tsp / 2 x 5 ml spoon *elychee* (cardamom)
2 lbs /900 grms granulated sugar
2 large tins (800 mls) evaporated milk
2 ozs /15 grms grated ginger (optional)
2 large pieces cinnamon sticks
4 litres water

Method
- Boil sugar and water with cinnamon sticks.
- Heat *ghee* on a slow fire and add flour.
- Keep stirring flour until parched (or until the flour is loose).
- Add cream of wheat, raisins, *elychee* and grated ginger.
- Add *phaag* (sugar mixture) and milk.
- Turn briskly with a *dabla* (wooden spoon) until light and fluffy.
- Allow to cool before serving.

Serves 40-50 persons.

Variations
Some cooks in the Caribbean use condensed milk as an additional ingredient. Others prefer to use cream of wheat alone while some use flour. This recipe, however, uses both flour and cream

of wheat. In Guyana, essence and nutmeg are used in the making of *parsad* while *elychee* is rarely used and cream of wheat is not used at all.

hand mill

Paynuse

Traditionally, paynuse *has been made from the milk of a cow that has just given birth. Today powdered milk is more commonly used. Even up do this day,* paynuse *is not available for sale because it is made at home and is considered a rare delicacy.*

Ingredients

1 lb / 450 grms powdered milk
½ lb / 225 grms brown sugar
1 ¹/6 pts / 700 mls water
2 sticks cinnamon
2 ozs / 50 grms grated ginger
Juice from 2 ripe limes

Method

•Mix powdered milk and water.
•Swizzle until there are no lumps left.
•Bring to the boil in an iron pot.
•Add cinnamon, grated ginger and sugar.
•Stir in lime juice.
•Keep stirring constantly on slow heat until brown.

Serves 6-8 persons.

1. Roat   2. Sohari   3. Panjaree   4. Halwa   5. Lupsee

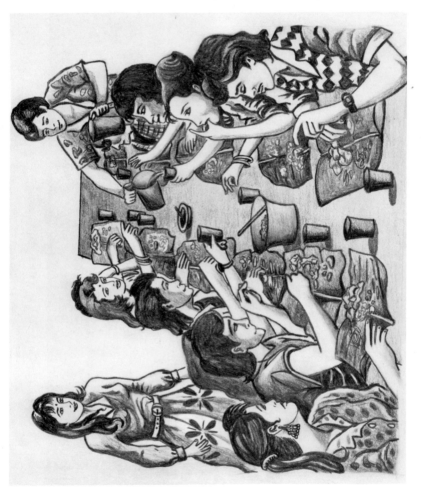

Guests eat with their hands on sohari leaves at a sumptuous Indian dinner in contemporary Caribbean

Pera

Pera *can be found with* ladoo *and* jalebi *in snack-packs at food stores in Trinidad. It is usually served to the guests at Hindu weddings.*

Ingredients
1 lb / 450 grms white flour
1 tin / 397 grms condensed milk
¾ lb / 350 grms granulated sugar
1 tsp / 1 x 5 ml spoon freshly ground *ginger*
1 tsp / 1 x 5 ml spoon ground *elychee* (cardamom)
¼ pt / 150 mls water
¼ litre /250 ml water (to knead flour)

For frying
¾ lb / 350 grms *ghee* (clarified butter) or
½ litre / 500 mls vegetable oil

Method
•Mix flour with water to form a stiff dough.
•Make into 3 *loyahs* (balls)
•Roll out *loyah* ¼" thick and cut into small strips about 2" long.
•Fry in *ghee* or oil until crisp and light brown.
•Drain on absorbent paper.
•Cool and grind very fine in a hand mill.
•Add sugar to ¼ pint water and boil until syrup spins a thread.
•Add remaining ingredients and stir.
•Mix in ground flour mixture and stir briskly.
•Spread mixture on a greased tray about ½" thick.
•Cut into squares while it is still warm.

Makes 2 dozen.

Rasgoola

This sweetmeat is usually served at Hindu weddings, but is not as popular as ladoo, kurma *and* pera.

Ingredients
1 lb / 450 grms powdered milk
8 tsp / 8 x 5 ml spoon white flour
2 tsp / 2 x 5 ml spoon baking powder
2/5 pt / 240 mls evaporated milk
½ litre / 500 mls vegetable oil

For Syrup
1 lb / 450 grms sugar
1 pt / 600 mls water
2 tsp / 2 x 5 ml spoon ground *elychee* (cardamom)
2 ozs / 50 grms grated ginger

Method
- Mix all the ingredients together except oil.
- Shape into smooth small balls (the size of a *phulowrie)*.
- Heat oil in a small iron pot.
- Fry balls until golden brown.
- Drain on brown or absorbent paper.
- Meanwhile, boil water and sugar to prepare syrup.
- Add rest of ingredients to syrup and stir.
- Remove from fire when syrup thickens.
- Add balls to syrup.

Makes 4 dozens

Serve with or without syrup.

Sawine

Sawine is served mainly during the Muslim festival of Eid-ul-Fitr. It is otherwise ideal for a dessert or a quick snack.

Ingredients
1 pack /212 grms vermicelli (fine noodles)
1 tsp /1 x 5 ml spoon butter
1 tsp /1 x 5 ml spoon *elychee* (cardamom)
1½ tins/596 grms condensed milk
2 ozs/50 grms raisins or currants (optional)
6 grains clove
2 medium size sticks cinnamon
1 tin /250 mls evaporated milk
2 pts /1200 mls hot water
Cherries, almond nuts, prunes (optional)

Method
- Put water to boil.
- Break up vermicelli into small pieces about 1 " long.
- Melt butter in a fairly large iron pot.
- Add vermicelli to butter and let it parch until it turns to a golden brown colour. Keep turning vermicelli.
- Pour all the boiling water in pot with the vermicelli.
- Add raisins, clove, cinnamon, evaporated milk, condensed milk and *elychee*.
- Allow to boil for a few minutes until tender.
- Serve with chopped nuts, cherries and prunes.

Serves 8 persons.

Variations
Some cooks in the Caribbean prefer not to use condensed milk; sugar is added when they use evaporated milk only. In Guyana, sawine is often made into cake forms which are cut and served.

115

Sweet Rice (Rice Pudding/Kheer)

Sweet rice has a unique flavour and is often eaten as a dessert. Some people enjoy it with daahl puri roti *as a meal. It is also eaten ceremoniously by the* dulaha *(bridegroom) during the Hindu marraige ceremony.*

Ingredients
½ lb /225 grms white rice
1 tin /397 grms condensed milk
8 -10 grains clove
4 pts /2400 mls water
1 tin /250 ml evaporated milk
1 tsp /1 x 5 ml spoon *elychee* (cardamom)
2 medium size pieces cinnamon
2 ozs /50 grms freshly grated ginger (optional)
2 ozs /50 grms raisins

Method
• Bring water to boil.
• Pick and wash rice and add to boiling water.
• Add cinnamon and clove.
• Allow rice to boil until soft.
• Add ginger, condensed milk and evaporated milk.
• Stir frequently to prevent rice sticking to the bottom of pot.
• Add *elychee* and raisins and continue stirring.

Serve hot or cold (*kheer* thickens as it cools).

Serves 10 persons.

Variations
In India, bay leaf is added to *kheer.* Some cooks in the Caribbean use granulated sugar, nutmeg, almond, vanilla and salt as additional ingredients. In Guyana, custard powder is added to thicken the *kheer.*

THE NUTRITIONAL VALUE OF SOME FOODS

Food & Measure	Weights Grms	Calories	Protein Grms	Fat Grms	Carbohydrate Grms
Chickpeas, dry, 4 ozs	114	408	23.2	5.4	69.2
Chives, raw, 4 ozs	114	32	2	0.3	6.6
Coconut, dried, unsweetened, shredded, 4 ozs	114	75	8.2	73.6	26.1
Eggplant, raw, 1 cup	398	50	2.4	0.4	11.2
Garlic, cloves, peeled, 5 average cloves	10	14	0.6	trace	3.1
Ginger root, fresh, 1 oz	28	14	0.4	0.3	2.7
Limes, fresh, unsweetened, 1 tablespoon	15	4	trace	trace	1.4
Mangoes, fresh, diced, 1 cup	163	108	1.1	0.7	27.4
Butter, 1 tablespoon	14	100	0.1	11.3	trace
Milk, cow's, fresh, 1 cup	244	159	8.5	8.5	11.9
Milk, dry, whole 1 tablespoon	7	35	1.8	1.9	2.7
Onions, mature, fresh, 1 average (2½" diameter)	110	40	1.6	0.1	9.6
Peppers, sweet, green, raw, 1 average	62	14	0.7	0.1	3

Potatoes, white, boiled, peeled, 1 small	100	65	1.9	0.1	14.5
Pumkin, fresh, pulp only, 4 ozs	114	30	1.1	0.1	7.4
Rice, brown, cooked, 1 cup	168	200	4.2	1	42.8
Sugar, brown. 1 cup	212	791	0	0	13.5
Sugar, granulated, 1 tablespoon	12	46	0	0	12
Yogurt, 1 cup	246	153	7.4	8.4	12.1

SOME PLANTS USED IN THE MAKING OF *BHAJI*

Poi/Indian spinach

Gooma

Sarhaachee/alligator weed

Nuniya/khursa/pursley

Marsa/chowrai/wild spinach

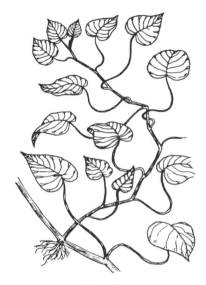

Karmi

Small sarhaachi/pani ni bhaji

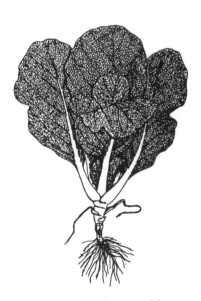

Pak choi/Chinese cabbage

ILLUSTRATIONS OF OTHER EDIBLE PLANTS

Amrak/bilimbi/cucumber tree

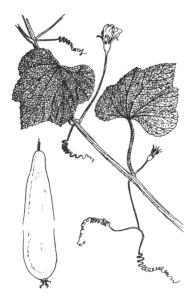

Lowkee/bottle gourd

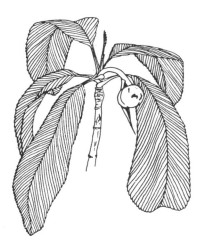

Chalta/elephant apple

Jinghee/angled loofah

GLOSSARY OF COOKING TERMS

bake to cook by dry heat usually in an oven.

batter a mixture of liquid, flour, etc., that can be beaten or stirred.

baste to moisten food while baking or cooking by pouring liquid or fat over it.

beat to make a mixture smooth and to introduce air by brisk regular motions that lift the mixture over and over.

combine to mix ingredients.

condiments food seasonings such as salt, vinegar, herbs and spices.

cream to blend foods until soft and fluffy, usually applied to shortening, butter and sugar.

dice to cut into small pieces.

dough a mixture of liquid, flour etc., that is stiff enough to be handled or kneaded.

dust to sprinkle lightly with flour or sugar.

fry to cook in fat.
deep fry - to cook in enough fat/*ghee*/vegetable oil to completely cover food while cooking.

grate to reduce to small particles by rubbing with anything rough and indented.

grind to reduce food to particles.

knead to manipulate with a pressing motion using your hands while folding and stretching, usually applied to bread and *roti* dough.

marinade	an oil and acid mixture as french dressing in which food is allowed to stand to give flavour to meats and salads.
mince	to chop very fine.
mix	to combine any manner that effects distribution.
parch	to cook by means of dry heat.
sauté	to cook in a small quantity of fat.
simmer	to cook in a liquid at a temperature below boiling point, save for a few stray bubbles to indicate that the liquid is sufficiently hot to extract the juices and flavour of the food being cooked.
stir	to mix by using a circular motion - widening the circles until ingredients are blended.

GLOSSARY OF HINDI TERMS

aam chatni	mango chutney
aloo	potato
anchar	hot spicy pickle
bandhara	religious ceremony observed on the 12th day after the death of a person
barahee	celebration observed on the 12th day after the birth of a baby
belna	rolling pin
besan	flour made by grinding dried chick peas
bhaji	the cooked tender leaves and shoots of dasheen, pak choi, spinach, etc.
chalni	wooden or metal sieve for straining liquids and for sifting flour
choka	vegetables roasted or boiled and pounded with spices
chowkee	breadboard for rolling out dough to make *roti,* pastry or bread
chownkay	to add uncooked food in hot oil or vice versa
chulha	a fireplace using dry wood for cooking
chutney	bitter-sweet sauce, usually made from sour fruits
daahl ghotnee	stick to swizzle split peas
dabla	a wood pallet used for cooking
dahee	yogurt; sour milk
goglet	clay jar for storing liquids to keep cool

jharnaa/jhanna	a long-handled spoon with a perforated disc at the end; normally used for draining food items out of a deep fryer
kalchul	a deep spoon with a long handle for lifting liquids
kuchilla	shredded hot pickle made from mangoes or pomme cythérès and preserved with mustard oil and pepper
loyah	dough made into a round ball
lorha	round stone for grinding
lota	brass cup without handles
methai	sweetmeats
munaka	currants or raisins
musar	wooden pestle
okhree	wooden mortar for pounding grains
parsad	usually made of flour and clarified butter, but means any oblation
partan	dry flour for dusting when making *roti*, bread, etc.
phaag	a mixture of sugar and water boiled to form a syrup
poran	spices and flavourings burnt in hot oil to which food is added
puja	Hindu ceremonial worship
puchara	a piece of stick with strips of cloth tied to the end for applying / basting oil on *roti*
roti	flat, round bread
sabji	vegetables
sil	flat grinding stone

simthaa /chimta	a pair of long tongs; normally used for picking up food items from direct heat; usually used in cooking *sada roti* in a *chulha*
talkari	curried vegetable
t(h)ariya	a wide brass plate
tawa	a cast iron or aluminium griddle, available with or without a handle for making *roti*

RECIPES: ENGLISH INDEX

RECIPES: INDIAN INDEX

About the author

Kumar Mahabir received his Ph.D. in Medical Anthropology from the University of Florida. As a doctoral student, he won a Florida Caribbean Institute Award, an A. Curtis Wilgus Fellowship, and an Organisation of American States (OAS) Fellowship. Dr. Mahabir has published six (6) books including the national best-seller **Medicinal and Edible Plants used by East Indians of Trinidad and Tobago.** He has also published several articles in scholarly journals including the **New West Indian Guide, Caribbean Studies, Florida Journal of Anthropology** and the **Toronto South Asian Review.**

OTHER BOOKS BY KUMAR MAHABIR

The Still Cry: Personal Accounts of East Indians in Trinidad and Tobago during Indentureship (1845-1917).
1985. 191pp. ISBN 0-911565-03-5. TT $50. US $25.

The reports of five surviving ex-indentured immigrant labourers are recorded verbatim to read like an epic poem. A woman, a Madras emigrant, a Muslim, a Brahmin and a cocoa/rubber estate worker narrate the conditions of life in village India when they left, the trauma of crossing the *kala pani* (black water), and the experience of adjusting to a new life among strangers and under a driver and overseer in the plantation ranges of the New World.

A Dictionary of Common Trinidad Hindi.
1990. Third impression. 44 pp. TT $20. US $10.

This illustrated dictionary contains more than 1,200 Indic/Hindi items which were in common usage in the plural society of Trinidad at the time of collection. The items had entered the Trinidad Creole by the process of cultural diffusion.

Medicinal and Edible Plants used by East Indians of Trinidad and Tobago.
1991. Third impression. vi + 166 pp. ISBN 976-8001-73-9. TT $40. US $20

This book contains valuable information on sixty-five local plants, each of which is illustrated, described and given a botanical name. Their medicinal uses include arthritis, diabetes, high blood pressure, headaches, strokes, impotence, sterility, ulcers and skin infections.

East Indian Women of Trinidad & Tobago: an annotated bibliography with photographs and ephemera..
1992. vi + 346 pp. ISBN 976-8012-76-5. TT $50. US $25.

This is the first book in the Caribbean which provides information on 236 successful Indian women. The 218 annotated references are accompanied with 130 carefully chosen photographs, some of which are in colour.

Order your copies by calling 1 (868) 674-6008 or by posting money order/cheque to Chakra Publishing House, Swami Ave., Don Miguel Rd., San Juan, Trinidad W.I.
E-mail: kumarmahab@hotmail.com

Healthy Cooking

Use Bragg's Apple Cider Vinegar

in all your vinegar recipes. It's the #1 food recommended for maintaining the body's digestion and vital acid-alkaline balance. Use it in your salads, peppersauce, for pickling or just as a cocktail drink.

BRAGG'S LIQUID AMINOS

This is your perfect health alternative to Tamari and Soy Sauce. It brings new taste to your salads, soups, tofu, veggies, rice and beans, potatoes, bhagi, gravies and sauces.

Try it, you'll love it!!!

Are you allergic to dairy products or simply lactose intolerant? **RICE DREAM RICE MILK or SOY DREAM SOY MILK** can be used as a beverage or with cereals, but has been included in a large variety of cakes, recipes and milk based punches over the years. It's a definite joy for those just wanting to replace milk due to allergies and indigestion or simply those wanting a healthier lifestyle. Available in Original, Vanilla and Chocolate .flavors.

Compliments: Health Food Specialists Limited. No. 19 Forres Avenue, Cocoyea Village, San Fernando. Trinidad. .Tel: (868)652-0684 Fax: (868) 653-7045 Email: healfood@carib-link.net.

DUMPLING MIX

The Taste of Tobago

Ingredients: Wheat Flour, Corn Flour & Cassava Flour

Processed & Packaged by
Sultana Foods.
Email: gmarket@tstt.net.tt

Commitment to High Quality Products

BRAVA INTERNATIONAL LIMITED

Medicinal & Edible Plants

Kumar Mahabir

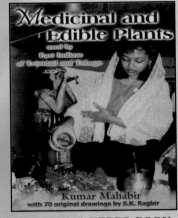

This book contains valuable information on sixty-five (65) plants used mainly – sometimes exclusively – by the East Indian community of Trinidad and Tobago. Their uses range mainly from medicinal – arthritis, diabetes, headaches, strokes, impotence, sterility, ulcers, skin infections, etc. and culinary - *talkari, chutni, kuchila, dhal,* etc, to miscellaneous values. Each plant entry is accompanied by an original drawing for easier identification.

**Order copies by communicating to
Chakra Publishing House (Caribbean)
LP 52, Swami Avenue,
Don Miguel Road,
San Juan, Trinidad and Tobago,
West Indies.
Tel (868) 674-6008, 675-7707.
E-mail: kumarmahab@hotmail.com**

MEDICINAL HERBS BOOK
6 x 9 paperback. Approx 169 pages
TT$45 or US$25
(includes handling & postage)
Second Edition 2001
ISBN 976-8001-739012-75-7